Ice and Fire

Avoiding the ice of discouragement
Fanning the flame of encouragement

Mike Mellor

©Day One Publications 2019

First printed 2019

ISBN 978-1-84625-646-2

A CIP record is held at the British Library

Published by Day One Publications, Ryelands Road, Leominster, HR6 8NZ

☎ 01568 613 740

FAX 01568 611 473

email—sales@dayone.co.uk

web site—www.dayone.co.uk

Cover design by Kathryn Chedgzoy

Printed by 4Edge

To my dear wife Gwen,
Fellow soldier and companion through many a battle

What a thrill and a privilege to read Mike's book! It comes like an inspiring song of praise which will stir our faith and set hearts aflame. It is just what many in complacent churches or discouraging circumstances need today. Paul told Timothy he needed to fan God's gift into flame. I think if Mike's book had been around in those days, the apostle might well have bought a copy for his young friend and said, 'Read this!'

Dr John Benton, Director for Pastoral Support for the Pastors' Academy, London Seminary

An incredibly timely book which thrilled and haunted me in equal measure. This is a must-read for a naive generation of Christians who have not faced up to what we must expect if we're to take up our cross and follow Christ. I found it profoundly inspiring to see how both Bible figures and our forebears faced suffering and persecution from both inside and outside the church, and I am so grateful that this material has been pulled together to prepare us for the days ahead.

Rico Tice, Senior Minister, All Souls Church, London, and co-author of *Christianity Explored*

It's easy to become discouraged and fearful in the face of pressure and hostility. Our own weaknesses and struggles can quench our passion for Christ and his kingdom. Ice and Fire is a timely reminder that God's people can persevere with faith and courage because of the unquenchable power of the Holy Spirit who lives within us. Following in the footsteps of faithful brothers and sisters, we can run towards 'the prize for which God has called us heavenwards in Christ Jesus' with joyful *anticipation and assurance. This book will inspire us to run faster!*

Carolyn Lacey, author and speaker

Everyone involved in Christian work has experienced the showering ice of discouragement. It is always tempting to give up, but when we are made aware of who is holding the bucket, we realize that this is what we must expect. Drawing from the Scriptures, the experiences and writings of those who have gone before, and his own personal experience, Mike Mellor makes us fully aware that we are engaged in a battle against an enemy who is the master of the art of deception, and that one of the most potent weapons in his armoury is 'the master weapon of discouragement'.

The author makes it abundantly clear that an awareness of the cause of discouragement is not enough, but points us to the 'flame God lights by the Holy Spirit in the hearts of men and women which, no matter how hard they may try, men and demons—even our own folly and unbelief—cannot extinguish'. Using mini-biographies and illustrations taken from the lives of God's servants, Mike stokes the fires that burn dimly in the lives and ministries of those who are facing discouragement. My one regret from reading this excellent book is that it was not in my hands the day I set out in the Christian ministry.

Dr Jim Winter, holder of a PhD in pastoral psychotherapy and after thirty years in pastoral ministry now with an itinerant ministry, lecturing and preaching in the UK and South East Asia

Acknowledgements

Thanks to Jim Winter for his gracious encouragement; to Sharon James for her helpful suggestions; to Roger Carswell for his more than generous Foreword; and to the countless saints through the years who have helped to keep the fire burning in times of discouragement.

Contents

Foreword by Roger Carswell

Christians have not been commissioned to discuss theology whilst drinking lattes. We have not been sent to give flip-flops to weekend revellers. We have not been commanded to organize community events. These may all be legitimate, but we have been commissioned to go into all the world and preach the gospel.

Our instructions are clear, and yet Coca-Cola and McDonald's leave us standing when it comes to effectiveness in making an impact. We have God on our side, Jesus as our Lord and Saviour, and the Holy Spirit Himself enabling us, yet we are often intimidated into silence concerning the gospel. We have the most wonderful message in the world: that 'Christ Jesus came into the world to save sinners', yet often we are too fearful to share it with close friends and neighbours, as well as those with whom we come into contact in everyday life.

The greatest act of kindness we can show anyone is to introduce them to Jesus. And the greatest act of tyranny is to know the good news of Jesus and yet not pass it on.

Millions of men and women—in the UK and in other lands—are lost. They are without Christ, and so without hope. In a hundred years' time they will be in eternity. Heaven and hell are real, and apart from Jesus there is no other name under heaven whereby people can be saved. Wycliffe Bible Translators have a song: 'Every person, in every nation, in each succeeding generation has the right to hear the news that Christ can save.'

Mike Mellor's conversion to Christ is a powerful demonstration of God's unchanging ability to save. His Christian life and witness since then have overflowed with the love of Jesus. So when Mike writes about evangelism, we are reading an authentic voice, which has been schooled in Scripture and ministry.

Ice and Fire is true to its author and all that the Lord has done for him. Mike helpfully diagnoses the pressures which are on all who say they love the Lord and want to evangelize. We are human and face fears and discouragements, but *Ice and Fire* is like a blowtorch designed to evaporate those icy notions which turn us away from being the people we know we should be.

The potted biographies in the 'Fire' section of this book serve as a tonic to kindle renewed spiritual heat. Biography is scriptural, and inspirational. I found myself underlining and marking quotations and whole paragraphs as I read this book. I know I will be going back to it time and again.

I thank the Lord for Mike Mellor: his zeal challenges me; his warmth encourages me; his passion stirs me; and his writings are always a blessing.

The last line of the Wycliffe Bible Translators' song is: 'Father, I am willing to dedicate to thee life and talent, time and money; "Here am I, send me."' I pray that *Ice and Fire* will be used by God to lead us all to pray like that. Only then will we be able to obey the Great Commission and reach our generation for Christ.

Roger Carswell
Yorkshire-based evangelist

Introduction: 'Fire and Ice'

Some say the world will end in fire,
Some say in ice.
From what I've tasted of desire
I hold with those who favor fire.
But if it had to perish twice,
I think I know enough of hate
To say that for destruction ice
Is also great
And would suffice.

(Robert Frost, 1920)

In his short poem 'Fire and Ice', the American poet Robert Frost sketches the familiar topic regarding the fate of our fragile earth. He poses the question as to whether it is more likely to be destroyed by fire or by ice—the point being that both are equally powerful. The poet, however, does more than describe two mere impersonal elements; he personifies them, associating fire with desire and passion, whilst connecting ice with hatred and hostility. He portrays both not only as immensely powerful, but also as devastatingly destructive. Thought-provoking as the poem is, it comes as an enormous comfort when one realizes that our planet, and those who inhabit it, is not in the hands of unpredictable elements or impersonal blind fate, but is under the care and supervision of its wise Creator and Sustainer, who will have total control over its demise, just as He had over its conception.

A WORLD TO BE SAVED

In this book, I use fire and ice a little differently. Both forces are still massively powerful, but one is treated positively and the other negatively. One has the power to redeem; the other, the potential to destroy.

Therefore, the book is divided into two parts:

- Ice: the discouragements that come to the people of God in their efforts to live for Christ and make Him known to a world that stands in desperate need of hope and salvation.
- Fire: the encouragements God gives in order to save the world through His Son, in the power provided by the agency of the Holy Spirit.

PART 1

Ice

1 Surviving the ice-throwers

If this man were a prophet, he would know who is touching him and what kind of woman she is—that she is a sinner. (Luke 7:39)

Now Mr Morrison, do you really expect that you will make an impression on the idolatry of the Chinese Empire? (Words of a long-forgotten ice-thrower)

Do you remember the 'Ice Bucket Challenge' that not so long ago swept the world? In order to promote awareness of ALS disease (also known as motor neurone disease and in the USA as Lou Gehrig's disease), a bucket of ice and water was hurled over a person's head or other part of the body. All, of course, was cheerfully endured for the sake of a good cause. But when we think of phrases such as 'an icy stare', 'a frosty reception', 'frozen out' and 'the cold shoulder', we know only too well the withering negativity they express, as we have all been on the receiving end of such behaviour at one time or another. Surely, nothing douses enthusiasm and passion like a shower of icy water.

But where it matters most is in the spiritual realm, and whenever anyone starts to get passionate, fiery for Christ and His kingdom—watch out for the bucket of ice! Ice and fire can never co-exist for long. As we look at what is happening in the West and trace our rapid descent—from a Christian to a post-Christian and now heading at breakneck speed to an anti-Christian culture—discouragement can easily grip us. We need the proverbial 'healthy dose of realism' in order to recognize that pressure and opposition are the norm for us, and that at times like this, greater faith and courage are called for in order to retain perspective in our fire-dousing age.

TOO SOON TO QUIT!

Robert Morrison, Scottish pioneer missionary to China, laboured there for twenty-seven years with just one furlough home. The impact of Morrison and his co-workers was colossal. Foundations for educational and medical work were laid that would significantly impact the culture and history of the most populous nation on earth. But a bucket of ice was thrown upon him at an early and crucial stage of his mission, and could well have been the means of extinguishing his godly fervour. Shortly after his arrival in China, he was asked by one who should have known better, 'Now Mr Morrison, do you really expect that you will make an impression on the idolatry of the Chinese Empire?'

'No, sir,' replied Morrison, 'but I expect that God will.'

Morrison was determined to continue, but those cruel, insensitive words could have made him feel like packing the whole thing in. And that is just the effect a shower of well-aimed ice can have. When did *you* last feel like throwing in the towel? At those times—and we all get them—the thoughts flood in: 'I've had enough.' 'What is the point?' 'I'm done here.' 'What more can I do?' No doubt the young pioneer missionary felt as if he'd been punched in the stomach. The reality was, however, that he was feeling birth pains, not death pains. God was with him and for him, because there is always hope for the man or woman who is willing to press on in faith and humble dependence. 'The one who calls you is faithful, and he will do it' (1 Thes. 5:24). *Hudson Taylor* followed Morrison some years later, and said, 'God uses men who are weak and feeble enough to lean on Him!' In other words, there is divine power and provision available to those who seek to serve God despite their flaws, fears and felt weakness. But how many men and women are there who have set out full of holy ardour, only to have it quenched—whether over the course of a few significant minutes or prolonged dousing over many years? It comes as a particularly devastating blow to one just setting out in Christian ministry unprepared for the dousing to come upon him from *within* the church, from those expected to be a source of encouragement.

LEAVING SO SOON?

It could have been in the *Guinness Book of Records* for the shortest pastorate ever. I still blush with embarrassment when I recall tendering my resignation to the church deacons on my very first morning.

The previous day had been glorious. The large, packed Welsh valley chapel rang with praise, as well-wishers from churches near and far attended, swelling the congregation far beyond its normal size for my Induction Service. But the next day would be altogether different. Eleven o'clock came and the church was filled with anticipation, if not with large numbers. Ten minutes passed, and the members of the congregation waited. Fifteen minutes, but still no pastor or deacons had emerged from the vestry. I admit that it was one of those incidents throughout my years of ministry that I regret and would re-run if it were at all possible. After praying for God's blessing upon the service, the senior deacon had quickly run through the proposed order of service, then, fixing me with his eye, closed with the words, 'And we finish at twelve o'clock.' One didn't need a degree in maths to calculate that the time allotted to my first sermon before the church would be minimal. On the surface, it seemed a minor issue, and with more maturity I would, no doubt, have handled the matter differently. But I detected that behind those words lay something more than helpful guidance for the service. It was the ice bucket—and only the first of many I would receive in the years following. However, after eventually retracting my hasty words (and resignation), I entered the pulpit for my first efforts in pastoral ministry. As *Dr Raymond Edman*, former missionary to Ecuador and beloved Professor of Wheaton College, wisely and frequently said, 'It's always too soon to quit.'[1]

It is perhaps significant that we were to see more fruit for our labours in this area of service than in any other throughout the years of ministry that followed—although, of course, God alone is qualified to measure 'success'.

HIGHER AND HOTTER

One might well ask, 'How on earth is it possible to keep going, year after year, in the Christian life if we are in constant danger of having the life and fire extinguished—not only by the ungodly, but even by those in the church?' *John Bunyan* (1628–1688), in his classic *The Pilgrim's Progress*, demonstrated perfectly how it is that we are sustained:

Then I saw in my dream, that the Interpreter took Christian by the hand, and led him into a place where there was a Fire burning against the wall, and one standing by it, always casting much water upon it, to quench it; yet did the Fire burn higher and hotter.

Then said Christian, What means this?

The Interpreter answered, This Fire is the Work of Grace that is wrought in the heart; he that casts water upon it, to extinguish and put it out, is the Devil: But in that you see the Fire notwithstanding burn higher and hotter, you will also see the reason of that. So he had him come around to the back of the wall, where he saw a Man with a Vessel of Oil in his hand, of which, he did also continually cast (but secretly) into the Fire.

Then said Christian, What means this?

The Interpreter answered, This is Christ, who continually with the Oil of His Grace maintains the work already begun in the heart: By the means of which, notwithstanding what the Devil can do, the souls of His people prove gracious still. And in that you saw, that the Man stood behind the wall to maintain the Fire; this is to teach you, that it is hard for the Tempted to see how this Work of Grace is maintained in the soul.[2]

In this vivid illustration, Bunyan's Christian receives yet another invaluable lesson in the house of Interpreter, as he sees a fire burning against a wall and someone standing by it relentlessly throwing water on it, seeking to douse it. And yet, despite all his efforts, the fire continues to burn 'higher and hotter'. Christian is puzzled because, from his perspective, the fire has no chance of surviving the watery onslaught. However, whilst he marvels at the sight of the roaring flames, Interpreter takes him around the wall for a behind-the-scenes glimpse, and there he sees a man with a vessel continually fuelling the fire with oil. That man is Christ, Interpreter explains, who continually revives and sustains the soul of His faithful ones with grace, by means of the Holy Spirit.

There are three great lessons for us here:

1. Expect to be doused.
2. Expect God to provide you with sufficient grace.
3. Keep looking behind the wall!

God's grace will be sufficient for every temptation and trial, and He is able to provide copious supplies of the Spirit in order that you may live for Him and serve Him, even in the most difficult of situations. We can be encouraged that the fire will burn 'higher and hotter'.

But first we need to look at the power behind the ice-throwing, and then at some real-life scenarios, so that we can be forewarned and forearmed!

Notes

1 Quoted in Warren W. Wiersbe, *Too Soon to Quit!* (Fort Washington, PA: CLC Publications, 2010), p. 7.

2 John Bunyan, *The Pilgrim's Progress* (Edinburgh: Banner of Truth, 1977), p. 29.

ICE AND FIRE

2 The ice king and his kingdom

For our struggle is not against flesh and blood . . . (Eph. 6:12)

What greater encouragement can a man have to fight against his enemy, than when he is sure of the victory—before he fights—of final victory? (Richard Sibbes)

Although it might seem strange to speak of God's arch adversary as the ice king, the truth is that one of the most devastating effects satanic opposition can have upon Christians and the church is that of quenching holy fire and desire. Whilst we will not dwell here on the history of Satan's fall and the wide range of his enmity and malevolent activities, we do need to be utterly convinced of his purpose, power and potential to harm. In fact, the Scriptures haven't much to say about his origin and descent from a holy, perfect angel to one of total evil (Ezek. 28:12–17; Isa. 14:12–15; Luke 10:18), but they do speak clearly and copiously of his character, work and ultimate defeat.

There are two things that are absolutely essential for us to grasp:

- This powerful fallen being is diametrically opposed to all that God is and does.
- It is he who—whether directly or indirectly—is behind every hindrance to the work of God in the world and in the life of every follower of Jesus Christ.

His venom against the people of God in particular is made plain in Revelation 12. He is 'the great dragon', 'that ancient snake called the devil, or Satan' who was 'hurled down . . . to the earth, and his angels with him' (v. 9). We read that he is 'filled with fury', fully aware that 'his time is short' (v. 12) on earth. So, although he is powerful and mightily effective in 'lead[ing] the whole world astray' (v. 9), his ultimate and focused hatred is against 'those who keep God's commands and hold fast their testimony about Jesus' (v. 17). It is these, those whom Christ has redeemed and pardoned, that he constantly opposes and accuses (v. 10) and would destroy, given the chance. Not without reason does Scripture name him Apollyon—the destroyer (9:11). *John Bunyan* again graphically reminds us of the cosmic conflict in which every Christian is personally involved: 'Then Apollyon broke out into a grievous rage, saying, I am an enemy to this Prince; I hate his Person, his laws, and people; I am come out on purpose to withstand you . . . Apollyon flew at him, throwing darts as thick as hail.'[1]

FANTASY OR REALITY?

Of course, we are dealing here with things that are unmistakably and unavoidably supernatural—things that the man on the street would gladly accept, even enjoy, on Netflix; but for real? Even we who hold the Scriptures to be God's inspired, infallible Word, and our rule for life and practice, are living in a twenty-first-century material world and constantly have to battle unbelief.

Dutchman *Abraham Kuyper* was not only an influential and highly respected theologian, but also a perceptive journalist and politician. Although Prime Minister of the Netherlands (1901–1905), he was not embarrassed to state that there were powers at work in our world beyond those which could be seen:

If once the curtain were pulled back, and the spiritual world behind it came to view, it would expose to our spiritual vision a struggle so intense, so convulsive, sweeping everything within its range, that the fiercest battle ever fought on earth would seem, by comparison, a mere game. Not here, but up there—that is where the real conflict is waged.[2]

Perhaps for us all, the problem is that we are creatures of extremes, and the enemy of our souls is only too aware of this. Twentieth-century academic and author C. S. *Lewis* stated it well: 'There are two equal and opposite errors into which our race can fall [about 'the devils']. One is to disbelieve in their existence. The other is to believe, and feel an unhealthy interest in them. They themselves are equally pleased by both errors, and hail a materialist or magician with the same delight.'[3]

Of course, as evangelicals, we would all subscribe wholeheartedly to the existence, personality and power of the devil. But our perception of his activity may well vary, perhaps according to our individual personality and make-up. Some of us are more phlegmatic: we don't get over-emotional or too excited about things. We are solid and stable, not likely to go overboard spiritually, and perhaps we hold this 'warfare' thing at a distance: 'God reigns, Christ has conquered, Satan is a defeated foe. We just need to get on with obediently living the Christian life.' But, on the other hand, there are those who are more emotional by nature and perhaps *are* more at risk of 'going overboard'. Either way, the enemy of our souls knows how to play us, and has been seducing saints for thousands of years—with an enormous amount of success. Thankfully, he can never snatch away the salvation of a genuine child of God, but he labours endlessly to do the next best thing: to rob us of the *joy* of our salvation, which is the strength of our Christian life (Ps. 51:12; Neh. 8:10), or to have us ruin our testimony, thereby taking us out of the game altogether. But this foe is never more effective and successful than when flying beneath the radar and allowed to work in elusive, subtle ways.

EXPECT RESISTANCE

Anyone who buys an airline ticket does so with the acceptance that they could possibly experience a degree of turbulence at some point when in the air. Similarly, anyone embarking upon the Christian life does so with the understanding that they are not guaranteed a turbulence-free passage. In fact, Jesus made it clear to His followers that 'In this world you will have trouble' (John 16:33). The Greek word used here for "trouble" is *thlipsis* and it is translated in various ways in the New Testament: trouble, afflictions, anguish, distress, persecution. Our Saviour is graciously filling out for us in a little more detail what it means to take up our cross and follow Him. Negative as it might be viewed in some quarters, this is New Testament Christianity, and it is therefore vital that we are not caught out. We are to expect resistance in the Christian life and in the work of the gospel, seeing it as the norm, not the exception. The apostle Peter encourages us as

Christ-followers, 'if you suffer for doing good and you endure it, this is commendable before God. To this you were called, because Christ suffered for you, leaving you an example, that you should follow in his steps' (1 Peter 2:20–21).

SIGNING UP FOR WAR

Becoming a disciple of Jesus Christ means signing up for war, and the enemy essentially is three-fold: the world, the flesh and the devil; as someone once described it, the world around us, the flesh within us and the devil above us. Of course, there is a continual care to be exercised when speaking about the devil and his works. We should perhaps talk about our foe in a similar way to how we should report terrorism and terrorist activity: we don't want to give too much publicity and attention, yet we dare not fail to warn of the dangers. The apostles saw warning the churches of the devil's aims and activity as basic and essential teaching. Paul, for example, strongly urges us to

Put on the full armour of God, so that you can take your stand against the devil's schemes. For our struggle is not against flesh and blood, but against the rulers, against the authorities, against the powers of this dark world and against the spiritual forces of evil in the heavenly realms. Therefore put on the full armour of God, so that when the day of evil comes, you may be able to stand your ground, and after you have done everything, to stand. (Eph. 6:11–13)

Then Peter seems to aim to protect his hearers from surprise or any potential self-pity: 'Dear friends, do not be surprised at the fiery ordeal that has come on you to test you, as though something strange were happening to you' (1 Peter 4:12). He is pressing home the point that experiencing opposition is the normal Christian life. The heartening fact is that these trials will actually serve to strengthen, not weaken, our faith. Jesus Himself revealed to His disciples the bad news that tribulation awaited them, but immediately gave tremendous assurance by saying, 'But take heart! I have overcome the world' (John 16:33). Mature believers understand this and, by God's grace, are able to welcome, even rejoice in, the hardships they face, accepting, as Paul says, that 'suffering produces perseverance; perseverance, character; and character, hope' (Rom. 5:4).

GROWING PAINS

I remember reading Bible teacher of the last century *F. B. Meyer* put it something like this: 'The Christian life often resembles the climb of a mountain range. In the early days you are at the base, you walk the fields and meadows. Then a little higher up through the firs and pines. Then gradually steeper onto the craggy cliffs and rock faces. Mountains are God's methods.' In this book we will look at different situations in our Christian life and experience: in this first part ('Ice'), the types of situations that are likely to get us down; and in the second part ('Fire'), how great saints of the past not only endured them, but were gallant overcomers who by their witness call us to follow their example. In the West, we work out our Christian lives in a culture of ease and self-centredness which proclaims loudly in many ways that if something negative happens to us, it must be harmful. That is the exact opposite to the New Testament spirit of triumph through adversity—the way of Christ and the cross. We must *expect* resistance at every single step along the way.

We are continually walking up a descending escalator, and standing still is impossible. Every step that you take in your efforts to live a holy, Christlike life will be resisted. Every step you take to win a person for Christ will be opposed. If you seek to assess progress or success by the number of your Facebook 'likes' or Twitter followers, you are going to be looking to social media for approval rather than looking up to God. Don't be surprised if the smallest shower of iced water (perhaps a lack of 'likes') threatens to paralyse you!

A HYPER-CUNNING ENEMY

Not for one moment must you forget that not only the church but you personally have one on your case who is stronger, cleverer and more committed than you. He takes no holidays, no days off. His success rate is phenomenal, having deceived and destroyed millions over thousands of years—and he knows you intimately! The apostle Paul sought to ensure that believers in his day were wide awake, 'in order that Satan might not outwit us. For we are not unaware of his schemes' (2 Cor. 2: 11). The knowledge and sophistication of our age has served only to blunt our awareness to the potential harm in this particular dimension. We live among atheists and earth-bound materialists who think that this subject is absolute madness. In our so-called 'enlightened age', belief in a daily spiritual battle is considered utter lunacy or an unwelcome throwback to the superstition of the Middle Ages. And this cynicism affects us more than we realize. Past generations, however, were only too aware of the importance of highlighting these matters. Puritan *Thomas Brooks* (1608–1680) wrote a book, *Precious Remedies against Satan's*

Devices, to equip the saints of his day. He introduces us to these 'precious remedies' by saying, 'Beloved, Satan being fallen from light to darkness, from heaven to hell, from an angel to a devil, is so full of malice and envy that he will leave no means unattempted, whereby he may make all others eternally miserable with himself.'[4]

THE DEVIL'S WILES

Perhaps the word 'wiles' is better than the modern translation of 'schemes'—firstly, because some schemes are good, but nothing the devil does is good; and secondly, because 'wiles' speaks more of the deception behind his evil efforts to ruin us. One of the prominent characteristics of the devil is that he is a liar. Denouncing the Jewish leaders who opposed Him, Jesus warned of the one controlling them, that 'there is no truth in him. When he lies, he speaks his native language, for he is a liar and the father of lies' (John 8:44). Satan is the arch-deceiver, the mind and power behind the occult, false religions and the cults, and in using any means and methods he can to '[blind] the minds of unbelievers, so that they cannot see the light of the gospel that displays the glory of Christ, who is the image of God' (2 Cor. 4:4). Scripture plainly states the extensive range of his malice. He is described as 'a murderer' (John 8:44); 'the evil one' (Matt. 13:19); 'the tempter' (Matt. 4:3); a 'thief' (John 10:10); 'a roaring lion' (1 Peter 5:8); a deceiving 'angel of light' (2 Cor. 11:14). His agenda is unmistakably clear: destruction at all costs. Damned eternally himself, he seeks to bring as many as possible with him to ruin. Although his guises are many, he is single-minded in his aim, which simply is the ruin of every being created by the God he abhors.

It is this highly intelligent, powerful and organized being who ultimately is behind the wrecked and ruined lives in our world that we see relayed nauseatingly on the multiplicity of our screens day after day. If Satan is not the cause directly, he certainly is indirectly, as it was his devious and malicious actions in the Garden (Gen. 3:1–5) that brought down the whole of humanity, barring them from the eternal presence, protection and blessing of their loving Maker.

THE MASTER TAILOR

Our focus, however, is, as previously stated, to concentrate on Satan's efforts to render *Christians*—the light-bearers—powerless and ineffective, resulting in their relegation to the ranks of The Great Demobilized. *Thomas Brooks* sees this cunning enemy like a master tailor:

Satan loves to . . . suit men's temptations to their conditions and inclinations. If they are in prosperity he will tempt them to deny God. If in adversity he will tempt them to doubt God. If their knowledge is weak he will tempt them to have low views of God; if their conscience is tender he will tempt them to legalism. If they are bold he will tempt them to presumption; if timid, to desperation.[5]

His activity against us is ceaseless. He knows your temperament, your strengths and your weaknesses exactly, and you can be sure he won't waste time tempting you with the same things he tempts me with. He never rests from plotting, luring, enticing and ruining. This should rightly alarm and disturb us, causing us to be vigilant and totally dependent upon the One who alone has strength to help us.

But there is one weapon of the devil's to be feared above all others.

Notes

1   John Bunyan, *The Pilgrim's Progress* (Edinburgh: Banner of Truth, 1977), p. 62.

2   Quoted in Daniel L. Akin, *Exalting Jesus in Daniel, Christ-Centered Exposition* (Nashville: Holman Reference, 2017), commentary on Daniel 10:1–21.

3   C. S. Lewis, *The Screwtape Letters* (London: Fount, 1991), p. ix.

4   Thomas Brooks, *Precious Remedies against Satan's Devices* (Edinburgh: Banner of Truth, 1968), p. 15.

5   Ibid., p. 16.

3 The master weapon of discouragement

'I have had enough, LORD,' he said. 'Take my life.' (Elijah, 1 Kings 19:4)

You fool! You will lose your life, and the lives of those with you if you go among such savages. (Words of another long-forgotten ice-thrower)

In *Shadow of the Almighty*, the 'Life and Testimony of Jim Elliot', his widow *Elisabeth Elliot* (1926–2015) recalls the time they came to the crucial stage in their efforts to reach the Auca Indians with the gospel. This notoriously dangerous unreached Stone Age tribe lived in isolation deep in Ecuador's dense rainforest.

The enemy of souls is not easily persuaded to relinquish his territory. Seeing that his authority was going to be challenged, he soon launched an attack on the challengers. Jim was beset with temptations such as never before assailed him, and that master weapon, discouragement—which to my knowledge had held no power over him since his arrival in Ecuador—met him at every turn. A gloom seemed to settle over his spirit in December, and there were battles being fought in which I could not share.[1]

Note the phrase used by Elisabeth Elliot, 'that master weapon, discouragement'. The enemy has a whole array of tools in his armoury, but the tool of discouragement will succeed where all others fail. And the strongest and greatest of saints have felt its power. Paul was no wimp, but it is obvious that the great apostle battled to fight off discouragement's icy grip. He was well aware that 'our struggle is not against flesh and blood' but that it ultimately is against 'the spiritual forces of evil in the heavenly realms' (Eph. 6:12). But the fact is that struggles almost always come in flesh-and-blood form and in real-life situations, so we need a continual awareness of our need of the Lord's presence and power at all times to keep us from sinking.

GOING UNDER

James Fraser was born to a prominent English family in London and was trained as both an engineer and a classical pianist. As a young man he came across a tract written to Christians urging them to give their lives to reach the lost in China. As a result, he went on to do an incredible pioneer work among the Lisu people of south-western China in the early part of the twentieth century. Knowing only too well from his own battles the importance of not 'going under', he wrote,

Each time your spirit goes under and faints in the trials which come to you, you lose mastery over the powers of darkness —i.e. you get below them instead of over them in God . . . the mastery over them depends on your spirit's abiding in the place above them, and the place above them means knowing God's outlook, God's thoughts, God's plans, God's ways, by abiding with Christ in God.[2]

THE FIGHT OF FAITH

We constantly have to fight the 'faith versus sight' battle, and even, at times, the 'faith versus common sense' battle. Yorkshire Methodist *James Calvert* (1813–1892) led a group of missionaries to the inhospitable islands of Fiji in order to reach the people with the gospel. The ship's captain considered this to be lunacy, having good reason to believe that if God's servants were to be invited for dinner it would be they themselves who would be on the menu. 'You fool! You will lose your life, and the lives of those with you if you go among such savages,' he pleaded. But Calvert's reply was one not only of absolute faith, but of sound theology and whole-hearted obedience: 'We died before we came here.'

But let us not for one moment think that such battles are to be fought only by missionaries, ministers and the 'professionals' in the church. No! Each and every follower of Jesus Christ is locked inescapably and unavoidably in the same cosmic conflict. Our circumstances may differ, but Christ's call to a bold, simple obedience is exactly the same for all. We do need discernment, however, to recognize when our faith is under attack. Overseas Missionary Fellowship spiritual war veteran *R. Arthur Matthews* put it like this: 'The attacks that are physical and come against us through our circumstances are only the symptoms of the very real hostility of the world rulers of the darkness under the prince of the power of the air. Our first call is to withstand these invisible enemies.'[3]

The key to avoiding discouragement's icy grip is to seek (without unhealthy obsession) to discern just when a certain situation in our everyday life is being used by the enemy of our souls to assault or undermine our faith. 'But,' you may ask, 'can't I glorify God in my discouragement? If so, then surely discouragement can be a good thing!'

DISCOURAGEMENT—NEVER GOD'S WILL!
We need it firmly fixed in our minds that it is never God's will

that we be discouraged. Whilst we must take the strongest possible stance against the prosperity heresy, which teaches that God never wills that His children be sick or poor, and that financial blessing and physical well-being are always God's desire for His own, we need to see discouragement as something altogether different. It is not that discouragement is necessarily a sin in itself, but, like temptation, it can often lead us into sin and away from God—if we allow it to get a grip on us. I remember being surprised at hearing *George Verwer*, founder of Operation Mobilization, say, 'I have never had a discouraging day in my life.' He then added, 'I've had many discouraging mornings, afternoons, nights, but never a discouraging day!' The important point he was making, of course, is that it matters how you *respond* when ice has been hurled at you or discouragement's cloud has settled upon you. Discouragement is an energy-draining and faith-sucking foe, and because of the latent, malicious powers that lie behind it, it must be dealt with urgently and radically, with the awareness that its grip upon you could prove calamitous.

SPIRITUAL DEPRESSION

John Bunyan captures discouragement perfectly in *The Pilgrim's Progress*, almost certainly writing from his own painful trial. Christian falls into the Slough of Despond, signifying a period of spiritual depression into which even the strongest saint may enter. But then, even worse, he begins to descend into despair. Bunyan illustrates this by Christian and his travelling companion, Hopeful, being thrown into a dungeon in Doubting Castle owned by that champion 'iced-water thrower' Giant Despair who (significantly) beats them daily without mercy. 'Your only way out is death,' he snarls, and then hands them a noose, a knife and a bottle of poison so they can do the deed. Even Hopeful appears to betray his name, saying, 'Indeed our present condition is dreadful, and death would be far more welcome to me than to remain like this forever.' But the pitiless giant presses, 'So why are you waiting? Make an end of yourselves!' Suddenly, Christian remembers that all the time he has had upon him a key called Promise. This key fits and unlocks all the gates, and they escape Doubting Castle. They are free![4] Of course, there are a large number of Christian believers who suffer from the kind of depression that cannot simply be 'shaken off', and it is vital to recognize those conditions that come under the mental health category. In those circumstances it is essential to seek help from medical professionals.[5]

However, let us be convinced in our own minds of the potential that discouragement has to strike at any believer at any time. But we must also draw comfort from knowing that we are able to trust in our faithful God in any situation in which we find ourselves, thereby having no good reason to remain passively bound in discouragement's gloomy dungeon. Let us imitate the faith of gracious Puritan *Samuel Rutherford* who said, 'When I am in the cellar of affliction, I look for God's choicest wine.'[6]

LOSS OF PERSPECTIVE

There are three reasons why discouragement can grip and then disable us: perspective, perspective and perspective— or, more accurately, *loss* of perspective. The liberating truth is that, although we may have no control over our circumstances, we do have control over how we view them. On some days, the ice-throwers can hurl their worst at us and have little effect. But there are those times when hurtful words, bad news, feelings of inadequacy, fears that our labours are ineffective and fruitless, or a variety of situations and circumstances we normally are able to cope with threaten to totally overwhelm us. It is at these times we can be sure that we are losing or have lost perspective. Little problems seem gigantic, encouragements seem trifling, the future hopeless, our life and ministry worthless—and, worst of all, God seems distant, uninterested or even against us. Our greatest need at times like this is for a fresh vision of God—of His majestic power, presence and purposes.

TIME OF CRISIS

If ever there was a man in need of a vision of God it was Ezekiel. He was in the pits. It was a time of *national crisis* for God's people. Having profaned the land and even their temple with their idols and abominations, they were now paying the price for having turned from the living God by being carried away to Babylon. The chosen people were now exiles in a dark, pagan land, whilst the land that God had given them lay devastated and in enemy hands. But it was also a time of *personal crisis* for this young man. He felt sure that God was calling him to serve as a priest, but now there was no temple, no priesthood. What is more, those to whom he sought to minister had no desire for God anyway. He was as useful as a fisherman in the desert. Homeless, unemployed, unwanted, he was totally downcast.

Walking alone, deep in thought and despondency, Ezekiel suddenly notices something that causes him to forget all earthly matters. An enormous dark thunder cloud appears, yet it is no ordinary cloud. As it draws alarmingly closer, he sees that it is surrounded by brilliant light. It approaches nearer and nearer, and in the cloud he sees fire and what look like glowing metal creatures flashing back and forth like lightning. There is no language adequate to describe what his eyes see, and similes indicated by the words 'like' and 'likeness' have to suffice. The fiery creatures alone would be terrifying, but above them he sees a throne and One seated on it who is all aglow. And everything changes in an instant. Gone are discouragement, depression, despair. Ezekiel, behold your God! Reality has arrived and perspective returns. Significantly, the throne is mobile, not stationary. God is not left behind in Jerusalem, but is wherever his people are. Ezekiel's situation has not changed, but his perspective has. He is powerfully reminded that God still reigns and is working out His purposes.

'REMEMBER, O MY SOUL'

It has been said that we should never forget in the dark what God has shown us in the light. Bible commentator *Matthew Henry* warmly applies to himself Ezekiel's encounter with God: 'Remember, O my soul! and never forget what communications of divine love thou didst receive at such a time, at such a place.'[7] Christian, if you happen to be in discouragement's dungeon right now, you need to remember that God has not forgotten you. He knows exactly where you are, He still cares for you— and He still reigns! The 'key' of God's promises still fits every lock in Doubting Castle and sets the prisoners free. No matter how dark your situation or how dead your feelings, don't give up turning to God's Word. The Holy Spirit is able to bring comfort and release at just the time when the voices of doubt and the devil may seem their loudest and most persistent. We need to remember the assurance that He will not break this 'bruised reed' or snuff out this 'smouldering wick' (Isa. 42:3), and that He is able and willing to restore a battered faith, that the sufferer may gain perspective and once again see faith's beautiful child—Hope.

THE QUICKEST ROUTE TO DISCOURAGEMENT

Of course, attacks don't only come to us from the outside. It is a fact that we can be our own worst enemy. The surest way to discouragement and depression is to continually focus upon oneself—by which I don't mean that necessary biblical self-examination, but that sinful obsession with self: How am *I* performing? How am *I* perceived by others? Am *I* being noticed? That is driven by the cancerous desire for approval, praise and preferment. To be free from it, however, is easier said than done, living as we do in a culture that is obsessed with self, fuelled continually by its addiction to social media and the instant gratification it can provide. It was *C. S. Lewis* who perceptively wrote, 'Christian humility is not thinking less of yourself; it is thinking of yourself less.' American pastor and theologian *Tim Keller*, in his liberating little gem *The Freedom of Self-Forgetfulness*, makes much of C. S. Lewis on this matter of pride and self-obsession:

C. S. Lewis in *Mere Christianity* makes a brilliant observation about gospel-humility at the very end of his chapter on pride. If we were to meet a truly humble person, Lewis says, we would never come away from meeting them thinking they were humble. They would not be always telling us they were a nobody (because a person who keeps saying they are a nobody is actually a self-obsessed person). The thing we would remember from meeting a truly gospel-humble person is how much they seemed to be totally interested in us. Because the essence of gospel-humility is not thinking more of myself or thinking less of myself, it is thinking of myself less.[8]

ODIOUS COMPARISONS?

The overemphasis upon externals in our age affects us much more than we would care to admit. The emphasis on image is enormous. The pressure—especially for preachers—to look and sound like the real deal is massive. We have the luminaries of the church coming to us via the Internet and through social media, and we rejoice in so much that is good—but we take a look at our paltry efforts, and slump. The means of encouragement can often be a double-edged sword. We are just not media material. How could we possibly have any impact when possessing 'the perfect face for radio', alongside fears that we struggle to impress even our own Sunday school kids? Yet, when we turn to Scripture, church history and Christian biography we are presented with an array of characters who make us feel almost normal.

If we look at the mighty leaders of the eighteenth century, we see the squint-eyed *George Whitefield*, and the dapper, diminutive *John Wesley*, of whom it was said, 'He could fall out with his own shadow.' In the next century we see one of the greatest Welsh church-planters, *Christmas Evans*, who had a glass eye! It is reported that halfway through his sermon his socket would fill up with fluid, so he would remove his eye, wipe it with a handkerchief and pop it in again!

Then, of course, the great apostle Paul, according to tradition, was no oil painting. One ancient writer describes him this way: 'He was a man small of stature, with a bald head and crooked legs, in a good state of body, with eyebrows meeting, and nose somewhat crooked.'[9] There were undoubtedly times when Paul would have heard the taunts of our cruel enemy whispering, 'Just look at you. Who on earth would listen to you?' He knew what it was to have 'conflicts on the outside, fears within' (2 Cor. 7:5). In his letters to the church in Corinth we see him having to deal with the divisions that were driven by pride. Revealing the secret of his incredibly bold humility, he tells them: 'I care very little if I am judged by you or by any human court; indeed, I do not even judge myself. My conscience is clear, but that does not make me innocent. It is the Lord who judges me. Therefore judge nothing before the appointed time; wait until the Lord comes' (1 Cor. 4:3–5). There was nothing of that brash 'I couldn't care what people think' attitude about the apostle. He knew what it was to feel the pain of being misunderstood, accused and unappreciated, and we mustn't think that somehow he was above having to do battle with discouragement. Far from it; there were plenty of reasons for him to want to quit. It must have been rather depressing, for example, for him to look at the church he had planted and see such dreadful behaviour—drunkenness at church meals, members suing other members, sexual immorality, some denying the resurrection—and on top of that to detect their boasting about how spiritually gifted they (the church in Corinth) were. But this man of God refused to allow himself to be overwhelmed by such displays of ice-throwing.

VICTORY IN PRAISE

There may well be occasions when a 'spirit of heaviness' comes upon us—perhaps due to pressing circumstances, or a 'cloud' may simply descend and remain for no apparent reason. At such times we need to look to Him who came

to comfort all who mourn,
    and provide for those who grieve in Zion—
to bestow on them a crown of beauty
    instead of ashes,
the oil of joy
    instead of mourning,
and a garment of praise
    instead of a spirit of despair [or 'heaviness', KJV].

(Isa. 61:2–3)

Whilst seeking to avoid a 'silver bullet' mentality in coping with such experiences, we have to admit that there often is inexplicable power and release to be found in God-focused praise.

Praise decentralizes self

Praise lifts us away from ourselves and our circumstances and concentrates our thoughts upon Him. Praise honours God, therefore God honours praise. Note how often in the Psalms the writer moves from lamenting to praising. In Psalm 31, for example, David seems to find sweet release from the burdens that weigh upon him and the snares that encompass him. We were created for worship, not worry; therefore, our souls thrive in gladness, not gloom.

Let us beware of being a slave to our feelings

'But I don't feel like it!' we so often object. However, our feelings have nothing to do with it. We *must* praise God! Praise is a sacred duty and privilege—a 'sacrifice' we are to 'continually' offer (Heb. 13:15). God expects His redeemed people to always bring Him praise and thanksgiving. 'I tell you,' said Jesus, 'if they keep quiet, the stones will cry out' (Luke 19:40).

Praise is a mighty weapon

In 2 Chronicles 20 we see the armies of Moab and Ammon making war against Israel. King Jehoshaphat calls on the people to seek God, and word is sent back, 'The battle is not yours, but God's . . . stand firm and see the deliverance the LORD will give you' (vv. 15, 17). As the people 'began to sing and praise' God, He dealt with the enemies that threatened to oppress them (v. 22). Praise was an essential ingredient in their victory, and victories still are won, and dark powers can still be put to flight, when God is praised. He is able to break the chains that bind us, remove the dark cloak of heaviness and give us the oil of joy in place of gloom and mourning.

Does sadness fill my mind?
A solace here I find,
May Jesus Christ be praised!
Or fades my earthly bliss?
My comfort still is this,
May Jesus Christ be praised!

. . .

The powers of darkness fear
When this sweet chant they hear:
May Jesus Christ be praised![10]

Music may be a help to us

C. H. *Spurgeon*, preaching on the text 'Now bring me a
minstrel' (2 Kings 3:15), spoke of the effect music can have
in bringing relief in times of darkness and oppression. Elisha
was passing through a particularly difficult period: 'The
prophet's spirits were depressed.' Spurgeon then spoke of
this being a common human experience, and how God has
provided a means of relief through music:

Our minds are disarranged, the machinery is out of order, the sail
is furled, the pipe is blocked up, the whole soul is out of gear . . .
'Bring me a minstrel,' said the prophet, for his mind was easily
moved by that charming art. Music and song soothed and calmed,
and cheered him . . . Among our own helps singing holds a chief
place; as saith the apostle, 'Speaking to yourselves in psalms and
hymns and spiritual songs, singing and making melody in your
heart to the Lord.'

Spurgeon continued, 'Note how he connects it with peace in
his epistle to the Colossians: "Let the peace of God rule in
your hearts . . . "'[11]

We need all the help we can get, so, to assist you in your
praise, use a good hymnbook (what could be better than the
Psalms!) or worship recordings. Praise God, no matter how
hard your heart feels or how oppressed your spirit may be.

WE DO NOT LOSE HEART

Standing like bookends at the beginning and end of Paul's

great chapter on ministry in 2 Corinthians 4 is the phrase 'Therefore, we do not lose heart' (vv. 1, 16). It is clear that he was often tempted to lose heart, but he tells us that the great motivation that kept him going like an express train, in season and out of season, was his eternal hope in Jesus Christ. He then spurs on those who share in that hope by concluding, 'So we fix our eyes not on what is seen, but on what is unseen, since what is seen is temporary, but what is unseen is eternal' (v. 18). *Thomas Brooks* said, 'Hope can see heaven through the thickest clouds.'[12] Because our hope is in Christ, it is a sure and certain hope; therefore we must continually 'fix our eyes on Jesus, the author and perfecter of our faith' (Heb. 12:2 NIV 1984).

In this way, we retain our perspective in this life of storms, blizzards and ice-throwers that threaten to overcome us. We need to recognize that this is the normal Christian life. Respected Bible teacher *John Stott* cautions us: 'The Christian's chief occupational hazards are depression and discouragement.'[13] This may be true, but we must never allow them to have the final word. That belongs to Jesus, so we must rest secure and satisfied in Him.

In Christ alone my hope is found,
He is my light, my strength, my song;
This Cornerstone, this solid Ground,
Firm through the fiercest drought and storm.
What heights of love, what depths of peace,
When fears are stilled, when strivings cease!
My Comforter, my All in All,
Here in the love of Christ I stand.

ICE AND FIRE

Notes

1 Elisabeth Elliot, *Shadow of the Almighty* (Bromley: STL Books, 1979), p. 243.

2 R. Arthur Matthews, *Born for Battle* (Sevenoaks: OMF, 1983), pp. 28, 29.

3 Matthews, *Born for Battle*, p. 25.

4 John Bunyan, *The Pilgrim's Progress* (Edinburgh: Banner of Truth, 1977), pp. 129–134.

5 It is essential to distinguish between the kind of discouragement that all have to contend with, and an ongoing depression that would indicate that one is among that company of people struggling with a mental health issue. There is no stigma attached to seeking health for an illness, whether physical or mental, and we must never think it a case of being 'weak in faith'. An extremely helpful book in this context is Dr Jim Winter, *Depression: A Recue Plan* (Leominster: Day One , 2000).

6 In I. D. E. Thomas, *A Puritan Golden Treasury* (Edinburgh: Banner of Truth, 2000), p. 17.

7 Matthew Henry on Ezekiel 1:1–3 in his *Commentary on the Whole Bible*, Bible Study Tools, https://www.biblestudytools.com/commentaries/matthew-henry-complete/ezekiel/1.html.

8 Tim Keller, *The Freedom of Self-Forgetfulness* (Leyland: 10 Publishing, 2012), pp. 31, 32.

9 *Acts of Paul* 3:3, in E. Hennecke and W. Schneemelcher, *New Testament Apocrypha*, vol. 2 (trans. and ed. R. M. Wilson; Philadelphia: Westminster, 1964), p. 354.

10 'When Morning Gilds the Skies', nineteenth-century German hymn, trans. Edward Caswall. Over the years, I have found that this hymn never fails to lift my heart towards God in praise and brings me release from heaviness:

1. When morning gilds the skies,
My heart awakening cries:
May Jesus Christ be praised!
Alike at work and prayer
I find my Lord is there:
May Jesus Christ be praised!

ICE AND FIRE

2. To God, the Word on high
The hosts of angels cry:
May Jesus Christ be praised!
Let mortals, too, upraise
Their voice in hymns of praise:
May Jesus Christ be praised!

3. Let earth's wide circle round
In joyful notes resound:
May Jesus Christ be praised!
Let air and sea and sky
From depth to height reply:
May Jesus Christ be praised!

4. The night becomes as day
When from the heart we say:
May Jesus Christ be praised!
The powers of darkness fear
When this glad song they hear:
May Jesus Christ be praised!

5. Does sadness fill my mind?
My strength in him I find:
May Jesus Christ be praised!
When earthly hopes grow dim
My comfort is in him:
May Jesus Christ be praised!

6. Be this, while life is mine,
My canticle divine:
May Jesus Christ be praised!
Be this the eternal song
Through all the ages long:
May Jesus Christ be praised!

11 Charles Haddon Spurgeon sermon, 'The Minstrel', 7 August 1881,
Metropolitan Tabernacle Pulpit, Vol. 27, The Spurgeon Center, https://www.
spurgeon.org/resource-library/sermons/the-minstrel#flipbook/.

ICE AND FIRE

12 In John Blanchard, *Gathered Gold* (Darlington: Evangelical Press, 1984), p. 152.

13 In John Blanchard, *Sifted Silver* (Darlington: Evangelical Press, 1995), p. 65.

ICE AND FIRE

4 Anticipating attacks

. . . in order that Satan might not outwit us. For we are not unaware of his schemes. (Paul, 2 Cor. 2:11)

The attacks that are physical and come against us through circumstances are only the symptoms of the very real hostility of the world rulers of the darkness under the power of the air. Our first call is to withstand these invisible enemies. (R. Arthur Matthews)

I have often thought that the Christian is rather like a rugby player, ball under arm, eyes steadfastly locked on the posts, running with all his might, whilst the opposition does all it can to prevent him reaching his goal. An arm here seeks to grab a leg, another there grasps round the waist, yet another seizes round the neck, but still he keeps striving doggedly ahead with all his might. By hook or by crook, we can be sure that men and demons will combine to bring pressure upon the saints with the aim of endeavouring to extinguish our holy fire and, if possible, causing us to buckle.

PHYSICAL HARM

We have an enemy who is incredibly adaptable. If stealth and deception will be most useful in a certain situation, he uses the more subtle approach. If the conditions are right, he attacks openly and ferociously. The apostle Peter warns, 'Be alert and of sober mind. Your enemy the devil prowls around like a roaring lion looking for someone to devour' (1 Peter 5:8).

As the sly serpent, he deceives. As the lion, he devours. So it is crystal clear that there is never a time when believers are 'off duty'; rather, they are always to be alert, clear-minded and vigilant.

The first Christians were to be on the receiving end of the roaring lion's venom, and subsequent church history is a record of the violent and persistent opposition against the church in this form. From the very start, the followers of Christ were 'out of step' with their idolatrous culture, and it wasn't long before they began to realize the truth of the Saviour's words, 'If they persecuted me, they will persecute you also' (John 15:20). This people, in seeking to be obedient Christ-followers, refused to conform to the accepted pagan customs, instead condemning the cruel public games, and refusing public office and the performing of duties such as burning incense to the gods.

As Christians, we seek to be loving, grace-filled members of the community; we strive to care for the poor and disadvantaged, and campaign for justice. The evidence of a fallen, broken world is all around us and we long to bring healing and hope. But such is the bias of the human heart that, although we may well have appreciation shown to us on occasion—or even receive an accolade or two—we will never really be accepted or trusted because of our bottom line.

SUSPICION

Our biblical stance inevitably arouses distrust and an animosity which, while usually concealed, may possibly break out in a moment. We are Christ's representatives, and we passionately seek to be a blessing to our increasingly needy communities, attempting to be both comforter and conscience to them. But at some point we may be in the position that our love is accepted but the truth we hold dear rejected. And there is always a price to pay for standing on the inflexible truth of God's Word. The apostle Paul found that the good news he brought to Ephesus and the blessing of transformed lives that followed brought condemnation upon him, not commendation. The consequences of his teaching led to a riot when the gospel affected the wallets of the inhabitants of the city—despite their clothing their avarice in the guise of seeking to defend the honour of their god. Not surprisingly, the early Christians were increasingly condemned as weird, intolerant and dangerous, and public opinion against them began to gather momentum, coming to an ugly head. The Roman historian *Tacitus* was an eyewitness to the first state-run persecution set up by Nero (AD 64–67) against the infant church. He wrote,

Therefore, to stop the rumour [that he had set Rome on fire], he falsely charged with guilt, and punished with the most fearful tortures, the persons commonly called Christians, who were hated for their enormities . . . In their very deaths they were made the subjects of sport: for they were covered with the hides of wild beasts, and worried to death by dogs, or nailed to crosses, or set fire to, and when the day waned, burned to serve for the evening lights. Nero offered his garden players for the spectacle.[1]

Amazingly, God has poured out extra grace and boldness upon His people at such times, thwarting such evil intentions aimed at destroying the cause of God. *Eusebius*, a godly fourth-century bishop of Caesarea, was threatened by Emperor Valens with confiscation of all his goods, torture, banishment and even death. His confident response was: 'He needs not fear confiscation, who has nothing to lose; nor banishment, to whom heaven is his country; nor torments, when his body can be destroyed at one blow; nor death, which is the only way to set him at liberty from sin and sorrow.'[2] It is the promise of Christ's presence, power and ultimate victory that has been the strength and motivation all through the history of the church. *Martin Luther* expressed this godly defiance well in his hymn 'A Mighty Fortress Is Our God' after recovering the true gospel, as he prepared for the worst, standing resolutely alone against the seemingly unassailable church of Rome:

And though they take our life,
Goods, honour, children, wife,
Yet is their profit small;
These things shall vanish all:
The City of God remaineth!

A PRICE TO PAY

It is that same clear perspective and courage that would so stir *Jim Elliot* centuries later that he could write in his diary those now-famous words, 'He is no fool, who gives what he cannot keep, to gain what he cannot lose.'[3] *John Foxe's* famous *Book of Martyrs*, first published in 1563, details the lives, sufferings and triumphant deaths of the early Christians, and then the Protestant Martyrs who followed. Among the many accounts of men and women who were willing to lay down their lives for Christ and His truth—some just young servant girls— are that of *Nicholas Ridley*, Bishop of London, and *Hugh Latimer*, Bishop of Worcester. Foxe describes the events leading up to their martyrdom, and then movingly captures their victorious departure from this world when they were burnt at the stake in Oxford on 16 October 1555. As the flames began to rise above them, the frail sixty-eight-year-old Latimer encouraged his companion with those memorable words, 'Be of good cheer, master Ridley, and play the man. We shall this day light a candle, by God's grace, in England, as I trust shall never be put out.'[4] Foxe's aim in recording the sufferings of Christians through the ages was not to engage in the morose and macabre; rather, he sought to show not only that God pours out extraordinary grace upon His faithful servants in their time of need, but also that the church of Jesus Christ is invincible, and that the 'candle' faithful Hugh Latimer spoke of was the inextinguishable flame of the gospel of Jesus Christ. The church of Jesus Christ is invincible, and though devilish powers do their worst, they will serve only to strengthen and even multiply this conquering company of redeemed men and women.

ROARING LION

The times when Christians were put to death for their faith in Britain may seem to belong to the distant past, but in more recent years the 'roaring lion' stirred 'regular' people to physically oppose those who dared to be on the offensive with the gospel. *The Salvation Army* in Britain—although now universally praised and accepted—experienced ferocious persecution in its early years:

- In Whitechapel, London, Salvation Army girls were pelted with burning hot coals.

- In Hastings, the town's leading grocer gladly offered supplies of rotten eggs to throw at them.
- In one year alone (1882), 669 Salvation Army soldiers were knocked down or assaulted.
- In Nottingham, one Salvation Army officer was beaten with a plank and lay unconscious for three days.
- One lady (one of William Booth's first converts) was kicked in the stomach and subsequently died.
- In Folkestone, roads were blocked to keep the Salvation Army out as they marched.

Police in those days admitted that they were powerless to protect the Salvation Army, so great were the mobs who were against them. Yet the Salvation Army exhibited tremendous courage. 'There is no place where The Army's women fear to enter, nor are the men less courageous,' reported Richard Harding Davis, a famous war correspondent of that time.[5]

It is not difficult to understand why founder William Booth named their weekly newspaper *The War Cry*. However, we dare not relegate to the past the 'roaring lion'-type of opposition to the church, as many of our brothers and sisters around the world are suffering terribly at this very moment. In 2015, 4,028 Christians—over 4,000 precious children of God—were killed for the faith in Nigeria. The Open Doors 2016 World Watch List showed a staggering 62 per cent increase in violent killings of Christians in northern Nigeria in one year.[6]

OPPOSITION INEVITABLE

As we seek to learn from church history and read reports from around the world in our own day, we must ask the question,

'Is there not something rather bland or anaemic about today's Western brand of Christianity that we incur so little spite from the enemy of men's souls?' God forbid that as followers of our gracious Saviour we should be brash or insensitive in any way. We cannot be too culturally aware and sensitive; we are to be wise like the men of Issachar, who 'understood the times and knew what Israel should do' (1 Chr. 12:32). We must not ignore the place that contextualization should have in our thinking: it is, surely, essential for any person seeking to communicate an idea or product to understand the minds and lifestyles of those they are seeking to reach and win; and the church is no exception here. We need to be continually labouring in order to present the gospel in a culturally relevant way, being fully aware that as Christians in our postmodern age we are all missionaries.

Yet the unescapable fact is that hostility towards our message, although bubbling beneath the surface for some while, has, these past few years, rapidly intensified and is now starting to erupt in a variety of ways, most noticeably in the area of sexuality and gender. Having been tolerated for so long, as Christians we feel ill-prepared for such blatant opposition and, if honest, seem to lack the strength and steel required in order to stand as we ought. There is also the danger that we take this animosity personally, as though we have not really taken on board the 'heads up' given by the Master, 'If the world hates you, keep in mind that it hated me first' (John 15:18). In the West, do we not have to admit that we are a 'slackened bowstrings' generation—geared up for leisure rather than war, or, at best, aware of the growing plight but still not equipped to deal with the powers *behind* those who are opposing? Yet this was not the case in past generations, for whom warfare was their daily occupation.

STRONG THROUGH THE STORM

After the Bible, *The Pilgrim's Progress* and William Gurnall's *The Christian in Complete Armour* were essential reading in the past, and were found on every Christian's bookshelf. *John Newton* wrote, 'If I might read only one book beside the Bible, I would choose *The Christian in Complete Armour*.'[7] In more recent days, Pastor *David Wilkerson* wrote in commendation of an updated reprint, 'I believe *The Christian in Complete Armour* . . . should be in the library of every man and woman of God. No Christian leader, teacher, pastor, evangelist, or Christian worker should be without it.'[8] The popularity of Thomas Brooks's *Precious Remedies against Satan's Devices* also reveals why past generations possessed such a rugged, steely faith. Such are the dark days approaching us that we surely need to adopt a more martial approach. *Open Doors*, founded in 1957 by Dutchman *Brother Andrew*, continues this day to be a remarkable source of help to persecuted believers around the world, providing Bibles, material needs, training, pastoral care and support in a variety of other ways. One such way has been their 'Standing Strong through the Storm' seminars to equip the church, helping to prevent God's people from being overwhelmed by the opposition encountered. *Dr Martyn Lloyd-Jones*, seeking to arm us for the battle, wrote,

I never tire of telling Christians to read the stories of the martyrs and the Confessors and the Protestant Fathers, of the Puritans and the Covenanters. Read their stories and you will find not only strong, courageous men, you will find weak women and girls and even little children dying gloriously for Christ's sake. They could not see it in themselves, but they were given a spirit of power.[9]

But such heavenly heroism is not confined to the past. In 2018, news came that the terrorist group Boko Haram in Nigeria had released all but one of the 100 kidnapped Dapchi schoolgirls. A fifteen-year-old Christian, *Leah Sharibu*, refused to convert to Islam, choosing cruel captivity rather than deny her Saviour. Leah's liberated classmates brought back her message to her mother: 'I know it is not easy missing me, but I want to assure you that I am fine. God is very close to His people in pain. I am witnessing this now. I am confident that one day I shall see your face again.'[10] Over a year has passed since then and her parents await news of their courageous daughter. 'I am very sad, but also very overjoyed because my daughter did not renounce Christ,' said her father.

HINDSIGHT, INSIGHT AND FORESIGHT
We stand constantly in need of this heavenly perspective. The apostle James writes, 'If any of you lacks wisdom, you should ask God, who gives generously to all without finding fault, and it will be given to you' (James 1:5). Thankfully, this is a wisdom that is from above and is freely given to all who ask, a heavenly perception provided in order that we might better understand God and His ways here on earth, in order to equip us with hindsight, insight and foresight. *Hindsight* is valuable as it helps us to learn from the past how previous generations of believers served God in their day and in their particular circumstances. *Insight* is gained from this, enabling us to

process what we have gleaned, in order to better understand our current situation and avoid unnecessary trouble, choosing our battles wisely. *Foresight* is that astuteness gained by walking humbly with God and studying His Word, equipping us with vision and strategies for the future. We are then a prepared people, clothed with hope and faith, and refusing to be overwhelmed by difficult circumstances. Hindsight, insight and foresight will ensure that we retain perspective and poise. We must avoid succumbing to that attitude of panic which tells us that we are sailing in uncharted seas, as we witness the approaching storm—a storm arising from a union of different factions who oppose us and our message, manifesting itself in multifaceted attacks against the church. This has been, and will continue to be, the story of the church as she obeys her Head by shining 'the light of the knowledge of God's glory' into a dark world where 'the god of this age' has blinded the minds of unbelievers (2 Cor. 4:4, 6).

SOVEREIGN LORD

In the book of Acts, we see the early church break out so powerfully upon the scene with their message of hope and healing that no reasonable person could deny something wonderful was happening. After the healing of a man crippled from birth, the religious leaders, although acknowledging it to be 'a notable sign' (Acts 4:16), came to the conclusion that they must deal robustly with those who appeared to be the source of the problem: Peter and John, the followers of that condemned Nazarene. Of course, because this was a devilish attack clothed in flesh and blood, 'they called them in again and commanded them not to speak or teach at all in the name of Jesus' (v. 18). The opposition knew just where to strike. Peter and John, however, realized the impossibility of obeying this command, utterly convinced that 'Salvation is found in no one else, for there is no other name under heaven given to mankind by which we must be saved' (v. 12; can there be a more offensive statement than that in any age?). After receiving further threats, they were released. But they then faced a real dilemma. Two conflicting commands rang in their ears: 'Go!'/'Stop!'; 'Speak!'/'Be silent!'

This is the ongoing story of the church, and the dilemma she will continue to face until the final day. We are often saddened but we ought never to be fazed by people and powers combining to war against Jesus Christ. We will never see the same collective hostility against followers of Buddha, Mohammed or Richard Dawkins. This is because Jesus Christ is God, and the heart of man, by nature, is at enmity with Him. 'But his subjects hated him and sent a delegation after him to say, "We don't want this man to be our king"' (Luke 19:14; cf. Rom. 8:7). *Abraham Kuyper* eloquently expressed the futility of their attitude: 'There is not a square inch in the whole domain of our human existence over which Christ, who is Sovereign over all, does not cry, Mine!'[11] But this is at the core of the bitter war that rages in our world.

THE GOD WHO FILLS

There is nothing like a common crisis to bring us together and squeeze our best and most sincere prayers from us. The atmosphere is too grave for boring, showy or polite prayers. We are blood-earnest at such times. Back in Acts 4, when that fragile little church received the news from Peter and John,

they raised their voices together in prayer to God. 'Sovereign Lord,' they said, 'you made the heavens and the earth and the sea, and everything in them. You spoke by the Holy Spirit through the mouth of your servant, our father David:
"Why do the nations rage
    and the peoples plot in vain?
The kings of the earth rise up
    and the rulers band together
against the Lord
    and against his anointed one."
'Indeed Herod and Pontius Pilate met together with the Gentiles and the people of Israel in this city to conspire against your holy servant Jesus, whom you anointed. They did what your power and will had decided beforehand should happen.'

(Acts 4:24–28)

Those who thought they were in a position of power had no idea who they were messing with. They had touched the apple of God's eye, His children, and now the kids had run back to tell Dad all about it!

'Now, Lord, consider their threats and enable your servants to speak your word with great boldness. Stretch out your hand to heal and perform signs and wonders through the name of your holy servant Jesus.' After they prayed, the place where they were meeting was shaken. And they were all filled with the Holy Spirit and spoke the word of God boldly.

(vv. 29–31)

Notice, firstly, that the fact that their enemies had banded together was no surprise to the church. Then, secondly, they didn't ask for the authorities to be removed, but rather prayed that God would empower His people to meet the hour. The Sovereign Lord obliged (after shaking the place) by filling them with the Holy Spirit so that they could '[speak] the word of God boldly'.

A VERSATILE ENEMY

Having recognized that there are powers and influences constantly at work seeking to take us out of the game, and being convinced that being pelted with the ice of discouragement is inescapable, it will be helpful now to consider the various ways that such attacks might come to us. Satan is no 'one-trick pony'. Perhaps the majority of the attacks we experience are subtle. But because of this, there is greater potential for our being caught off-guard—and the effects can be as distressing or devastating as those of overt attacks. A. W. Tozer comments, 'Failing in his frontal attacks upon the child of God, Satan often turns to more subtle means of achieving his evil purpose. He resorts to devious methods in his attempt to divert the Christian from carrying out the task God has committed to him.'[12] But whatever means or methods are used against us, it is imperative that we are always vigilant, ready and equipped, so that, as Paul urges, 'when the day of evil comes, [we] may be able to stand [our] ground, and after [we] have done everything, to stand' (Eph. 6:13). Thankfully, we have an enemy who, although versatile, is not that inventive, so we are able to learn from the various 'snares and scenarios' he has hatched and employed over the years, to help us gain the victory in our battles.

Notes

1 'Nero Persecutes the Christians, 64 A.D.', EyeWitness to History, http://www.eyewitnesstohistory.com/christians.htm.

2 Quoted at Grace Quotes, https://gracequotes.org/quote/when-the-emperor-valens-threatened-eusebuis-with-c/.

3 Elisabeth Elliot, *Shadow of the Almighty* (Bromley: STL Books, 1979), p. 110.

4 John Foxe, *Foxe's Christian Martyrs of the World* (Chicago: Moody, 1980), p. 482.

5 Quoted in Richard Collier, *The General Next to God* (London: Collins, 1962), pp. 94, 192.

6 A report released in Abuja by Open Doors and the Christian Association of Nigeria, 'Crushed But Not Defeated: The Impact of Persistent Violence on the Church in Northern Nigeria', makes a detailed study of the violence that has occurred.

7 Quoted in William Gurnall, *The Christian in Complete Armour*, Vol. 1 (Edinburgh: Banner of Truth Trust, 2017), p. 3.

8 Ibid., p. 16.

9 D. M. Lloyd-Jones, *Spiritual Depression* (London: Marshall Pickering, 1998), p. 102.

10 Open Doors magazine, May 2018, p. 4.

11 In James D. Bratt (ed.), *Abraham Kuyper: A Centennial Reader* (Grand Rapids: Eerdmans, 1998), p. 488.

12 'Satanic Diversion', The Alliance Tozer Devotional, 5 May 2017, https://www.cmalliance.org/devotions/tozer?id=802.

5 Snares and scenarios

. . . in all these things we are more than conquerors through him who loved us. (Paul, Rom. 8:37)

The reason why many fail in battle is because they wait until the hour of battle. (R. A. Torrey)

The love of Christ is the most powerful force in the world and can have an incredibly disarming effect upon even the most hardened of hearts. The evangelist *John Wesley*, during the years of his extensive ministry, was often opposed, at times violently, being pelted with stones, mud, excrement, even dead cats! He was a tidy, fastidious churchman who dressed immaculately in clerical robes, even though most of his ministry was conducted in the open air. Today, with our twenty-first-century penchant for pigeonholing everybody, we might classify him as obsessive–compulsive. And, no doubt, he would by nature have shunned having to preach whilst covered in mud, blood and crud. But the love of Christ so flowed through him that at times it could produce quite a remarkable change in the attitude of his adversaries. One day, as he stood on a chair to preach, yet another angry mob rushed towards him. He recorded in his journal, 'My heart was filled with love, my eyes with tears, and my mouth with arguments.' He then describes how a solemn hush came over the crowd: 'They were amazed; they were ashamed; they were melted down; they devoured every word.'[1]

ICE AND FIRE

PEOPLE NOT THE ENEMY

It is absolutely vital that we never see the 'ice-throwers' themselves as our enemies, but realize that it is the power behind them which is the real enemy. Paul reminds us of the importance of dealing with those who oppose us 'with gentleness. God may perhaps grant them repentance leading to a knowledge of the truth, and they may come to their senses and escape from the snare of the devil, after being captured by him to do his will' (2 Tim. 2:25–26 ESV). On those occasions when we are called to take the strongest of stands, love is to govern our every word, action and even look. Never are we to be in a place where we despise others, or feel the slightest animosity towards them. Hard as it may be in some situations, we are left no wriggle room in the words of our Lord Jesus: 'love your enemies and pray for those who persecute you, that you may be children of your Father in heaven' (Matt. 5:44–45). And such love surely is only possible by our being filled by the Holy Spirit. How important it is to be in no doubt that as God's people we are 'more than conquerors'—despite how we may feel at times by the 'snares and scenarios' that threaten to overwhelm us. But being aware of the form in which these attacks come upon us is vital, hence the reason for this lengthier chapter. Being forewarned and forearmed does give one a tactical advantage.

DISCOURAGERS

William Gurnall surely described the church at its most glorious when he said, 'The church is nothing but Christ displayed.'[2] If that is so, then the local church should be, as *Fred Catherwood* said, 'a community of encouragement'.[3]

Sadly, however, at times we have often found the church to be the very opposite (not that we ourselves can ever be in a position to plead 'not guilty' to a bit of 'ice-throwing'). There are times when, rather than receiving the encouragement we hoped for, the icy water of discouragement has been thrown our way.

Sadly, there are believers we encounter from time to time who seem to be particularly gifted in this area. When Scotsman *John G. Paton* was preparing to go as a pioneer missionary to the New Hebrides, an island chain north-east of Australia, a church deacon kindly offered him some inspiring words of reassurance: 'Cannibals! You will be eaten by cannibals!' The young man calmly replied: 'Mr. Dickson, you are advanced in years now and your prospect is soon to be laid in the grave to be eaten by worms. I confess to you that if I can but live and die serving the Lord Jesus, it will make no difference to me whether I'm eaten by cannibals or worms.'[4] Undeterred, Paton, together with his wife, Mary, sailed from Scotland in December 1857 and on 5 November 1858 landed on the island of Tanna in the New Hebrides for the start of what would be fifty-five years of fruitful missionary service. But it could have been an altogether story if the unthinking brother's words had been taken to heart.

Doing the devil's work

As disquieting as it may be to acknowledge, the Lord's people can unwittingly be used of the evil one. Our Saviour had no doubts as to the origin of Peter's words when he sought to deter Christ from going to the cross, forcefully responding, 'Get behind me, Satan! You are a stumbling-block to me; you do not have in mind the concerns of God, but merely human concerns' (Matt. 16:23).

The satanic powers constantly and vehemently active against Christ's messianic mission will use any means possible to achieve their ends, and what better instrument to use than the lips of others who also are employed to fulfil the Great Commission? In fact, the impact upon us can be all the greater when we receive discouragement or perhaps criticism from a believer. We expect it from those outside the kingdom, but when it comes from a fellow saint, the results can be devastating, especially if it hits us at a time when we are at our lowest and most vulnerable.

A young pastor can be especially susceptible. He commences a new ministry bursting with ideas and enthusiasm, only to be met by a cool, 'We've tried that, brother, it doesn't work' or similar quenching words. Another particular danger area can be church 'business meetings'. They often seem to bring out the worst in human nature if separated from an attitude and atmosphere of worship. In one of my pastorates, a church member addressed me in a meeting I was chairing, and with gritted teeth prefaced his sentence with the words, 'I say this in love, brother . . .' I realized from the white face and protruding veins throbbing on his forehead that I needed to brace myself for the words that were to follow. For this reason, in subsequent churches, our business meetings commenced with prayer, singing, Scripture reading and a brief message, designed as a reminder and aid to us all that worship is a 24/7 thing and that the Christian life is not compartmentalized.

SLANDER

Being misrepresented, misunderstood or the object of outright slander can be a particular trial.

There is an oft-told story, one that deserves being repeated, regarding *Susannah Spurgeon*, the godly, faithful wife of Charles. Susannah kept chickens but refused to give away for free any of the eggs they laid, insisting that everyone pay for them, even close relatives. This led to cruel gossip that the Spurgeons were mean and covetous. The couple, however, graciously accepted the criticisms without defending themselves, and it was only after Mrs Spurgeon's death that the truth was revealed. 'All the profits from the sale of eggs went to support two elderly widows. Because the Spurgeons were unwilling to let their left hand know what the right hand was doing . . . they endured the attacks in silence.'[5]

Our Saviour was cruelly labelled a glutton and a drunkard (Matt. 11:19), and Peter points to Him as the perfect example for us to imitate: 'When they hurled their insults at him, he did not retaliate; when he suffered, he made no threats. Instead, he entrusted himself to him who judges justly' (1 Peter 2:23). We must always seek to resist the temptation to spring to our own defence, and must remind ourselves that we are much worse than our accusers are saying, and be thankful that they don't know us better! At such times, we remind ourselves of the gospel we rest and rejoice in. As *Tim Keller* has often said, in various ways, 'We are more sinful and flawed than we ever dared believe, yet more loved and accepted in Jesus than we ever dared hope.'[6] This is our glorious position in Christ. Therefore, we must commit our reputation to the Lord; it is in His hands.

The power of meekness

It is when we are under such attacks that our humility and Christlike meekness are put to the test, so there is much potential for spiritual growth. *A. W. Tozer* wrote concerning this:

The meek man is not a human mouse afflicted with a sense of his own inferiority. Rather he may be in his moral life as bold as a lion and as strong as Samson; but he has stopped being fooled about himself. He has accepted God's estimate of his own life. He knows he is as weak and helpless as God has declared him to be, but paradoxically, he knows at the same time that he is in the sight of God of more importance than angels. In himself, nothing; in God, everything. That is his motto. He knows well that the world will never see him as God sees him and he has stopped caring. He rests perfectly content to allow God to place His own values. He will be patient to wait for the day when everything will get its own price tag and real worth will come into its own. Then the righteous shall shine forth in the Kingdom of their Father. He is willing to wait for that day. In the meantime he will have attained a place of soul rest. As he walks on in meekness he will be happy to let God defend him. The old struggle to defend himself is over. He has found the peace which meekness brings.[7]

Matthew Henry, commenting on the attack upon the character of Moses which had enormous potential in undermining his authority, points us to that great leader as a pattern of meekness; when he was under fire he was 'as bold as a lion in the cause of God, but as mild as a lamb in his own'.[8]

DEFECTORS

Another particularly painful area of discouragement to deal with is when those in whom we placed much confidence not only fail us, but seem to turn their backs on the only Saviour.

Paul's moving last words in 2 Timothy reveal just how much he had been let down by those who professed Christ, even by those who once were earnest fellow labourers in the gospel alongside him. His words have a heart-rending poignancy that reveals the vulnerability of even the greatest of saints:

> Do your best to come to me quickly, for Demas, because he loved this world, has deserted me and has gone to Thessalonica. Crescens has gone to Galatia, and Titus to Dalmatia. Only Luke is with me. Get Mark and bring him with you, because he is helpful to me in my ministry. I sent Tychicus to Ephesus. When you come, bring the cloak that I left with Carpus at Troas, and my scrolls, especially the parchments.
>
> Alexander the metalworker did me a great deal of harm. The Lord will repay him for what he has done. You too should be on your guard against him, because he strongly opposed our message. At my first defence, no one came to my support, but everyone deserted me. May it not be held against them. (2 Tim. 4:9–16)

When those in whom we have invested so much time, trust and emotional energy let us down, it comes as a double blow. We would recover more easily if let down or betrayed by an unbeliever, but when deserted or even opposed by one who once 'pulled the plough' alongside us, the cut is that much deeper and more painful.

'Shock, confusion and grief'

I recently received an email, earnestly requesting prayer, from friends of ours serving on the mission field in a Muslim-majority country. A man who had come to Christ, had been the means of bringing others into the kingdom and had then developed a considerable teaching ministry among his people, had become aggressive, engaging in deceit and even turning his back on his wife and two children. Our friends wrote, 'We have experienced shock, confusion and grief . . . some have even turned away from Jesus because of his actions. We feel grieved that we were not able to protect them . . . we are faced with the ugly truth that he has lied to us for a long time.'

There can be very few trials as painful for Christian workers as that, and when in the thick of them we can almost feel the hot breath of the enemy down our necks. *John Blanchard* reminds us, 'We are opposed by a living, intelligent, resourceful and cunning enemy who can outlive the oldest Christian, outwork the busiest, outfight the strongest and outwit the wisest.'[9] But as Paul continued writing to Timothy, we see plainly the source of his comfort in the midst of similar personal distress and disappointment: 'But the Lord stood at my side and gave me strength, so that through me the message might be fully proclaimed and all the Gentiles might hear it. And I was delivered from the lion's mouth' (2 Tim. 4:17). Although we may feel deeply hurt, let us not be surprised by such penetrating attacks. Satan works hard to make us believe that we have lived and served in vain, that we are nothing and that all our efforts will amount to nothing. For Nehemiah it was Tobiah the Ammonite who came saying sneeringly, 'What they are building—even a fox climbing up on it would break down their wall of stones!' (Neh. 4:3). Satan whispers cruelly, 'You are useless, all you have done is useless, your whole life has been pointless!' And there will be characters who will appear on the scene at significant times and be used by the enemy to shoot his fiery arrows. But the arch-liar knows only too well that Christ is building his church and that the gates of hell will not prevail against it (Matt. 16:18). At such times, we should take heart that the enemy views us sufficiently as a threat to pull out the stops to attempt to halt our work and impact.

The price of love

The very fact that we are committed and passionate beings will inevitably have a downside, too. To love God and others will of necessity mean that we make ourselves vulnerable. But, as *C. S. Lewis* eloquently points out, there really is no alternative for those who seriously seek to be like their Master:

There is no safe investment. To love all is to be vulnerable. Love anything and your heart will certainly be wrung and possibly broken. If you want to make sure of keeping it intact you must give your heart to no one, not even to an animal. Wrap it carefully round with hobbies and little luxuries; avoid all entanglements; lock it up safe in the casket of your selfishness. But in that casket—safe, dark, motionless, airless—it will change. It will not be broken; it will become unbreakable, impenetrable, irredeemable.[10]

We must be those of a more noble spirit who are able to love any who seek to oppose, harm or even destroy us. This, of course, calls for copious supplies of grace on God's part—and relentless determination on ours! 'I've made up my mind to love everybody—even if it kills me!' vowed the penetratingly honest *Tozer*.

FEAR

Fear, intimidation and mind games are classic weapons that Satan has used from the beginning. At a crucial stage in his efforts to restore the work of God, Nehemiah was vehemently opposed: 'our enemies said, "Before they know it or see us, we will be right there among them and will kill them and put an end to the work' (Neh. 4:11). Nothing can be more devastating than attacks upon the mind. Evil dictator *Adolph Hitler* often used these methods, boasting, 'Mental confusion, contradiction of feelings, indecisiveness, panic; these are our weapons.'[11] Our enemy is the arch-bully and he seeks to fill us with fear in order to render us paralysed and powerless. For this reason Paul wrote to timid Timothy, 'For God has not given us a spirit of fear, but of power and of love and of a sound mind' (2 Tim. 1:7 NKJV). Knowing our natural inclination to fear, our enemy will either create or cause us to imagine situations that threaten to freak us out.

Just as I write, a report has been sent from *New Foundations*, a medical mission working in Niger:

Our fifteenth year, we find our clinics shut, our workers distraught at the increase in infant deaths, and serious criminal activity scarring the creeks in which we work. Interior communities shield armed gangs and there's uncertainty who to trust. It seems that all that has been nurtured over the past years has fallen and remains in pieces. Our dear friend and partner in the work . . . has been taken from us (a violent abduction) and travel in the region is impossible for the foreseeable future. Cultic groups run community councils, the army swarms ineffectually over the waters and armed vigilantes stand waterside to protect villagers from night-time incursions . . . At least ten children dead in the past few weeks at E—, and more young lives at our satellite clinic, quite needlessly, families ripped apart by frustrated grief and suffering.

When Jesus was crucified and ascended he left, by human standards, a very poor business model—the oft-times misunderstood message of Salvation to a small rag-bag group of uneducated and unreliable followers. Yet the good news of salvation has spread such that Christianity still remains the predominant faith across the world, a message of love, hope and redemption, without coercion, threat of violence, ritual or good works.

Advice has been to employ armed escorts, to leave or to move elsewhere where needs are equally matched. To do so would be to acknowledge that outcome is all. The true testimony of the work has always been in the constancy of the Mission and in the resolute proclamation of the Gospel, and the love of God for His people. Occultic beliefs have experienced a resurgence in recent years. We have testimony of many corroborating factors like this. Paul's writings of a spiritual battle and the necessity for the 'whole armour of God' is so apposite for tackling these oppressive forces, and we have witnessed first-hand the power of God during our captivity . . . We continue to believe that only the Gospel preached without compromise, without shame or apology will meet these challenges head on, for Jesus is able. He is the same yesterday, today and forever, delivering the radical transformation of sinner to saint.[12]

The great temptation in our times of stress is to run ahead in our minds, forgetting our Lord's clear words 'Do not worry . . .' that come to us three times in the space of nine verses (Matt. 6:25–34), and his warning not to peek into what might happen tomorrow. He promises us grace for today, so let us focus on that space of time from now until midnight tonight, refusing to give in to that ever-hovering spirit of fear. 'Worry has an active imagination, and it can envisage all sorts and kinds of possibilities,' warns *Dr Martyn Lloyd-Jones*.[13] Once again, we dare not eliminate or underestimate Satan's interest and activity when it comes to our own personal temperaments and situations. Please don't for a moment think that you are somehow exempt from the battle and may fly under the radar.

Fighting talk

Nehemiah, in the midst of similar pressure as that of our friends in Niger, and armed with the same insight, boldness and faith, encouraged and stirred the people of his day, saying, 'Don't be afraid of them. Remember the Lord, who is great and awesome, and fight for your families, your sons and your daughters, your wives and your homes' (Neh. 4:14). We see the same military attitude throughout the life of Salvation Army founder *William Booth*. In what was the final, and perhaps most stirring, of his many addresses, the octogenarian cried,

While women weep as they do now, I'll fight; while little children go hungry as they do now, I'll fight; while men go to prison in and out, in and out, I'll fight; while there is a poor lost girl upon the street, I'll fight; while there remains one dark soul without the light of God, I'll fight—I'll fight to the very end![14]

DISTRACTION

Ezra and Nehemiah were victims of the devil's schemes in different ways. Ezra, having returned to Jerusalem and seeking with God's people to rebuild the city, had to combat hindrances to God's work in the form of the enemy using the subtle but effective means of bureaucracy: 'Then the peoples around them set out to discourage the people of Judah and make them afraid to go on building. They bribed officials to work against them and frustrate their plans during the entire reign of Cyrus king of Persia and down to the reign of Darius king of Persia' (Ezra 4:4–5).

We see this same form of opposition employed in our day, when the authorities in certain situations can be too cowardly to openly condemn the Bible but will use devious means to attack Christians and their faith. Intimidation that results in discouragement is always an effective weapon of Satan. Of course, as we read on in Ezra, we see God thwarting the efforts of his opponents by causing the previous edict issued by King Cyrus to rebuild the temple in Jerusalem to come to light. Sooner or later, God will vindicate His faithful servants. However, even in a less threatening situation, the outcome can be one of inertia, with the work of God seemingly coming to a halt through distraction or interruption. One authority from the business world stated that 'Distraction is the biggest killer of success. It is loss of focus through distraction that is the main thing that prevents people succeeding.' Nehemiah had to strongly resist the ploy of distraction when he later returned to head up the building work in Jerusalem. God's zealous servant had to contend with threats, mocking and derision. But when these failed, the enemies resorted to distraction and diversion. Sanballat and Geshem sent a message, 'Come, let us meet together in one of the villages on the plain of Ono.' However, Nehemiah could see through their perverse plot: 'But they were scheming to harm me; so I sent messengers to them with this reply: "I am carrying on a great project and cannot go down. Why should the work stop while I leave it and go down to you?" Four times they sent me the same message, and each time I gave them the same answer' (Neh. 6:2–4) The key to perseverance and victory is to stay focused on the task and keep our eyes fixed on our Sovereign God, refusing to buckle, sticking to our divine commission in faith whilst praying in humble dependence as Nehemiah did, 'Now strengthen my hands' (6:9).

Wong Ming-Dao, a wise and godly Chinese pastor, spent many years in prison for his faith. The authorities told him to stop his publication, *Spiritual Food Quarterly*, or else 'take the consequences'. He stood firm and wrote: 'A soldier is trained for a thousand days; he is used only briefly. This was the time God wanted to use me, and on no account must I flee as we approached the battle.'[15]

LONE RANGERS

They tell us they are Christians, yet show little regard for the church, and have an uncanny ability to throw ice upon us from their lofty perch, in a manner that makes us feel inferior in our love for and commitment to the local church. These people seem to fall mainly into two groups: Hoppers and Stoppers. The Hoppers have tried every church in town, and every one of them has been found wanting, whether it's the poor preaching, dull worship, cold fellowship or tasteless coffee. More often than not, it's because they have been wounded in some way by an insensitive church member. These poor souls, of course, are never to blame, so they just (half-heartedly) keep on doing the rounds, hoping to find that perfect church. The Stoppers are those who don't even attempt to worship with others, and may even be proud of the fact.

I have found the benefits of engaging in open-air evangelism to be multifaceted. Besides being able to reach the lost, opportunities abound to be able to minister, by God's grace, to struggling saints. The aim in any such encounter is always to encourage them to be settled, committed members of their local church, to come under the authority of the leadership and actively seek to be a blessing to others in that fellowship. However, the Stoppers are a breed on their own, and one is forced to question if they really are Christians. The right method of dealing with them is usually a firm one.

I was recently approached in the street and informed by a 'saint' how much he loved Jesus. I enquired as to which church he belonged to.

'Oh, I don't go anywhere, brother,' he replied smugly.

'I see; so you love Jesus, but His bride stinks?' I countered.

If a Stopper stays around long enough, I remind him or her of the instruction about 'not giving up meeting together, as some are in the habit of doing, but encouraging one another—and all the more as you see the Day approaching' (Heb. 10:25). I also mention all the 'one another's in the New Testament. Sadly, my words usually seem to fall on deaf ears. The point is that we have another example here of professing Christians who come as ice-throwers and are very effective at dampening zeal. At such times, let us thank God for the privilege of belonging to an imperfect yet most precious assembly of people on earth, the church of Jesus Christ. And let us dwell much on the beautiful pictures Scripture gives us of the church, such as the Bride, Body, Flock, Family and Temple. Joseph Hall warned, 'There is no place for any loose stone in God's edifice.'[16]

FAMILY AND FRIENDS
I believe it is here that we are most vulnerable. The closer we

are to a person, the greater the impact upon us negatively—as well as positively, of course. During that time of perhaps unparalleled calamity, his hour of greatest need, Job was deeply discouraged by the words and attitudes of his wife and friends. It's only fair, however, that we cut Job's wife some slack. When disaster strikes, she is suffering alongside her husband and shares with him in the dreadful loss of their children and family wealth. She watches in astonishment as her protector and provider sits desolate on a rubbish heap scraping his boils with a piece of broken pottery. What future do they have now? Out of sheer fear and exasperation she gives vent to her emotions and cries out, 'Are you still maintaining your integrity? Curse God and die!' (Job 2:9). But things were not going to improve for some while. Enter three theologically astute, verbally persuasive but pastorally bankrupt friends. They just don't get it. In the midst of his suffering and questioning of God, they try to be of help to Job, but just end up heaping more shame and blame on him for his afflictions with their woefully misapplied theology, leaving him comfortless and with nowhere to turn. Job replies pitifully, 'If only my anguish could be weighed . . . a despairing man should have the kindness of his friend . . . but my brothers are as undependable as intermittent streams' (Job 6:2, 14–15, NIV and Berean Study Bible). So there he sits, stripped in an instant of family, prosperity, dignity, health and hope, and—so he thinks—of the smile of the God whose favour he valued above all else. One desolate, heartbroken, guilt-ridden, sore-covered, throbbing mass of despair.

This long, forty-two-chapter account is in Scripture for good reason. There may well be occasions when we, too, feel let down in our darkest hour, even attacked by friends and family—the very ones we were counting on for support and encouragement just when it was needed most. Whether it is because they don't understand what we're going through or they fail to offer the help we hoped they might have, the outcome can be the kind of disappointment that quickly turns to bitter discouragement, and, if we are not careful, to deep, dark, brooding resentment.

Severe strain

But then, immense discouragement may come to us through the illness of a loved one who is greatly suffering, whether physically or mentally. Missionary to India *William Carey* carried the colossal ongoing burden of a desperately ill wife. Perhaps the tipping point for Dorothy came when their son Peter died of dysentery, which, along with other causes of stress, resulted in her suffering a nervous breakdown from which she would never recover. *John Marshman*, the son of one of Carey's fellow labourers (an eminent journalist and historian), records how Carey worked away on his studies and translations 'while an insane wife, frequently wrought up to a state of most distressing excitement, was in the next room'.[17] It was no secret that Carey's own wife was the greatest hindrance to the life's work he was called and committed to. One can only wonder how she might have fared had there been more awareness of, and help available for those battling with, mental health issues. She surely was a woman in desperate need.

Again, we must realize that our adversary the devil knows just where and when to strike, and the potential of being able to affect us through those closest to us, to such an extent that we can be overwhelmed on a personal level and, if sufficient passion-dousing 'ice' is experienced, may even need to leave our sphere of Christian service. If we are those who enjoy the support and encouragement of a faithful spouse, we should be ever reminding them just how important their sacrifice and support is to us, often labouring lovingly in the background caring for children and home whilst we are seen as doing the 'real work'. God, for sure, doesn't see it this way.

Our soul's rest

But it could be that you are one who is deprived of such comfort and support, and you can identify with Job only too well. Such times can be desperately lonely. But there is 'a friend who sticks closer than a brother' (Prov. 18:24). It is here, in the times of our deepest distress, that we must turn to the One who alone knows our inmost needs and frustrations, and who alone is able to pour comfort and hope into our souls and give grace to enjoy a life of usefulness. We can do no better than turn to the Psalms and, using the anguished cries of those who have been in similar situations before us, make them our own.

Out of the depths I cry to you, LORD;
  Lord, hear my voice.
Let your ears be attentive
  to my cry for mercy. (Ps. 130:1–2)

Truly my soul finds rest in God;
  my salvation comes from him.
Truly he is my rock and my salvation;
  he is my fortress, I shall never be shaken . . .

Yes, my soul, find rest in God;
   my hope comes from him.
Truly he is my rock and my salvation;
   he is my fortress, I shall not be shaken.
My salvation and my honour depend on God;
   he is my mighty rock, my refuge.
Trust in him at all times, you people;
   pour out your hearts to him,
   for God is our refuge. (Ps. 62:1–2, 5–8)

As a brand new Christian, I discovered with utter relief and surprise that I could simply get on my knees, lift up my heart to heaven and pour out to God the innermost burdens of my soul—even if I was unable to express myself in words. Only shortly afterwards, through reading the eighth chapter of Romans, did I learn that it was the Spirit helping me in my weakness, interceding for me through my wordless groans (Rom. 8:26). Never must we forget that we have an all-sufficient, ever-present Saviour in our Lord Jesus. *William Gurnall* encourages us, 'And if the fight should be too much for you, your dear Saviour stands by with reserves for your relief at a moment's notice. His very heart leaps within Him to see the proof of your love and zeal for Him in all your combats.'[18]

UNSAVED LOVED ONES

The concern, and at times conflict, that can come through having unsaved loved ones can be another wide-open door through which discouragement can pour into our lives. Furthermore, the thought of them being lost eternally can—if we allow it—prove an almost crushing sorrow. Incredibly, Jesus had to contend with the pain of having family who (at that time) did not understand or believe him: 'For even his own brothers did not believe in him,' the apostle John records (John 7:5). And if those we love leave this life without Christ (as far as we are humanly able to discern), we simply have to entrust them into the hands of our all-compassionate, all-wise God. 'Will not the Judge of all the earth do right?' (Gen. 18:25). But whilst they are in this world, we must never give up loving, praying and seeking to speak to them of the Saviour, never losing sight of the fact that God is able to break into their lives at any time and completely turn them around.

Betty was a gracious, faithful Christian married to Dilwyn, who was a good man, a paramedic, yet humanistic and atheistic in his outlook. He 'did his bit' for society and was 'pleased for Betty' that 'her religion did her good'. When I visited their home, Dil would usher me into the lounge and then politely leave me to do the 'religious bit' whilst he moved on to more practical, manly matters. One couldn't help feeling wimpish as Dil, a broad-shouldered six-footer, left the room. However, I began to discern a gradual change in him after he was diagnosed with a life-threatening illness. This keen gardener started to linger when I visited and made comments about how there must be 'Someone behind the scenes' who gives life, makes things grow, and so on. As time passed, Dil would hover around and then stay in the room as I read the Scriptures and prayed with Betty. My wife and I invited them both to our home for dinner, and a friendship developed—albeit a short one, as not long afterwards he was taken into hospital a very ill man. Even then, I did not expect Betty's call that was to bring the good news:

'Hello, Pastor!' chirped the excited Welsh valleys voice on the telephone. 'Dil has come through!'

My mind being elsewhere, as I was in the middle of sermon preparation, I thought, 'Come through what? His greenhouse glass?'

'He has trusted the Lord!' Betty continued.

Of course, I expressed how pleased I was, yet, as I put the phone down, I was inwardly grappling with how God could be so gracious to someone who had not yet come to church on a Sunday! But 'come through' Dil most certainly did, as during his remaining weeks on earth he showed a genuine love and gratitude for the One who had loved him and given His life for him. One factor that cannot be left out, however, is that Betty had prayed for her stubborn husband for *over forty years*! So don't give up on those in whom, at present, you see no encouraging outward signs. Keep on patiently loving, trusting and praying.

But perhaps there is no greater pain than that of a parent of a prodigal son or daughter. We need to remind ourselves continually that they are never out of the reach of our prayers. In chapter 8 we will see how the prayers of a heartbroken mother were wonderfully answered. Her prodigal son, who for years had been held in the grip of rebellion and immorality, was not only wonderfully saved, but was raised up to become a mighty champion for the church of Jesus Christ. Never must we forget that 'with God all things are possible' (Matt. 19:26), and that He is not uninterested or aloof, but is with us and for us in this.

CRITICISM

What in this world could be more mind-blowing than to know that we are loved by Almighty God, the Creator of all things—'Loved with everlasting love, led by grace that love to know', as Wade Robinson put it in his hymn. Yet we have to admit that, despite having every reason to be a people with poise and gracious confidence, we can at times be pathetically insecure and defensive, who don't take kindly (to put it mildly) to being criticized. But criticism is inevitable. Sometimes it may seem harsh and unwarranted, other times it may be just what we deserve and actually need. But rarely do we embrace it with open arms. Preachers, pastors and anyone else in church leadership will have felt the biting sting of criticism at some time or other. But how do we see it: as a friend or a foe? At first sight, we see it as a foe attacking us, taking ourselves much too seriously. Tim Keller writes, 'The biggest danger of receiving criticism is not to your reputation, but to your heart. You feel the injustice of it and feel sorry for yourself, and it tempts you to despise not only the critic, but the entire group of people from which they come. "Those people . . . ," you mutter under your breath.'[19]

So the potential for discouragement through criticism is enormous. But it need not be if we can turn 'the sword into a ploughshare', making the attacking weapon a means of growth and grace. The next time criticism comes your way, try to do the following:

- *Avoid* any knee-jerk reaction in either seeking to defend yourself or attacking your critic. Be aware of the pride within, being slow to speak and slow to become angry (James 1:19–20).

ICE AND FIRE

- *Respond* gently, remembering that a gentle answer turns away wrath (Prov. 15:1). This will take the heat out of the situation. Remember how gracious God is to us when we offend Him.
- *Pray* about the criticism, asking the Lord to reveal if there is any truth in it, and, if so, for grace to put right any wrong done or to change any attitude that needs changing (Ps. 139:23–24).
- *Recognize* this as an opportunity for growth, remembering God's sovereignty over all, even in allowing attacks upon your character. Joseph could say, 'You intended to harm me, but God intended it for good' (Gen. 50:20).
- *Thank* God that the one who criticized you doesn't know you better. We are much worse than our critics could ever imagine (Ps. 130:3).
- *Rest* in the fact that you are loved by God, whether at your best or at your worst. Seek His praise and approval above that of all others (1 Cor. 4:5).

Thomas à Kempis, the medieval monk, wisely wrote, 'He has great peace of heart who cares neither for praises or revilings. He will be content and brought to peace, whose conscience is clean. You are not more holy if you are praised, nor baser if reviled. You are what you are; nor can be called better than what you are in God's estimation.'[20] We need to cultivate that humility of heart which frees us from bondage to either criticism or praise, that state of humility which lifts us, as the Puritans quaintly said, 'above the frowns or flattery of man'. Deeply prayerful South African pastor and writer *Andrew Murray* (1828–1917) defined the lowliness that brings inner rest: 'Humility is perfect quietness of heart. It is to expect nothing, to wonder at nothing that is done to me, to feel nothing done against me. It is to be at rest when nobody praises me, and when I am blamed or despised.'[21] How liberating for a culture which lives under the tyranny of social media's smile or frown.

REJECTION

Few things we experience in life can cut as deeply as rejection—from being overlooked for a promotion or failing to be selected for a sports team, to the heartbreak of being unwanted as a child or deserted by a partner. Rejection can bring pain that penetrates to the very core of our being. But what comfort it brings when we realize that we have a Saviour who knows what it's like—that God Himself should have chosen to walk the thorny path of rejection for us: 'He was despised and rejected by mankind, a man of suffering, and familiar with pain' (Isa. 53:3). The pain He felt, however, must have been doubled. For not only was he saddened when people rejected Him personally, but He who was perfect in love was distressed by the knowledge that rejecting Him was rejecting life, salvation, heaven and everlasting hope. Surely, we, His followers who relay the good news of salvation to our generation, will know, at times, a similar heaviness of heart, even though we lack the depth of His divine compassion. In love, we come with a message that can change a person's eternal destination, only to be met with derision, hostility or, worse, indifference. Yet we have recorded for our sakes how the Son of God dealt with this gut-wrenching experience. Having been rejected by the Galilean towns in which He had so passionately preached and performed such astounding miracles, with heavy heart He lifted His face heavenwards, saying, 'I praise you, Father, Lord of heaven and earth, because you have hidden these things from the wise and learned, and revealed them to little children. Yes, Father, for this is what you were pleased to do' (Matt. 11:25–26). It is always hard having to cope with those who reject us, because they are rejecting the Christ whom we love and follow. It is especially painful for a young Christian.

Dan was a teenager in our church in the Welsh valleys who had to pay a price for following Jesus. His family resented his new way of life, and his father in particular gave him much grief, expecting his only son to follow the tradition of accompanying him to the miners' club to drink with the other men and their boys. 'What's wrong with you?' he would rage. 'Why aren't you out in the pubs and clubs at night like other lads your age?' Dan was showered with ice when he should have been showered with love.

Some burdens are simply too heavy for us to carry, so we must roll them upon the mighty shoulders of our Sovereign Lord. When the pain of rejection cuts, we remind ourselves that nothing can separate us from the Father's love. Even should the whole world be against us, if the God of the universe is for us and with us we shall have enough comfort and strength to continue. 'Consider him who endured such opposition from sinners, so that you will not grow weary and lose heart' (Heb. 12:3).

ILLNESS

The strongest believer is never far from moments of near

despair. We need a constant awareness that the most mature of saints, especially in time of illness, can be assailed by gargantuan doubts and fears, and may be a special target of the enemy of our souls when in a weak condition, whether physically or mentally.

When I was a newly converted Christian I went to the local hospital to visit a godly, mature saint whom I deeply respected and who had been unwell for some weeks. Before trusting Christ, *Gwynn*[22] had been a professional boxer in South Wales. He was now a radiant elderly believer who for many years had been fighting 'the world, the flesh and the devil' and had been a great encouragement to me in my spiritual infancy. For this reason, when I went to visit him in hospital I was staggered to discover that he was doubting his salvation. For me, a rookie in the faith, it was a powerful lesson that the godliest man or woman can be seriously assaulted by the enemy of our souls when ill and stand in need of another 'soldier' to draw alongside to remind them of those promises of God, which those of us enjoying good health would consider the most natural verses to turn to in times of doubt or weakness. Let us never underestimate the relentless diabolical efforts of our enemy.

A dear friend of mine was a passionate, godly and most effective preacher and evangelist whose life, and subsequent death through cancer, was one of joyful faith and obedience. His was a triumphant departure, but it was not without one last violent assault from the evil one upon the faith of this beloved child of God as the end of his life drew near. His wife graphically described the dreadful attack:

On the way to the hospice in the ambulance, Carl[23] suddenly grabbed my wrist really tight and with great panic and fear in his eyes, said, 'Mel,[24] I'm not saved—I'm not going to heaven.' I held his hand and tried to reassure him that he was, reminding him that God had given eternal life to those who have repented and believed in Him and His work on the cross for us—and that ETERNAL means FOR EVER. But he was in too much of a state to really listen. I prayed really hard that the Lord would help him, and I reminded him of one of his favourite verses from John 14 where Jesus had said to His disciples, 'I go to prepare a place for you.' 'But I don't know if it's prepared for me!' he shot back. I reminded him of the words just before, where Jesus said, 'If it were *not* so, I would have told you.' God answered my prayer and Carl became calm and sure of his salvation. I was reminded yet again, that praying and quoting God's powerful word made the devil flee. Praise God!

Carl died with joy and peace, but at such times of felt weakness or violent spiritual attack, saints stand in tremendous need of being reminded of both the compassion and the faithfulness of their Saviour, who 'a bruised reed he will not break, and a smouldering wick he will not snuff out' (Isa. 42:3), and who has promised, 'Never will I leave you; never will I forsake you' (Heb. 13:5). How essential it is that we stand upon the unerring Word of God at all times, but especially when it comes to leaving this life and entering eternity.

LIFE

Life itself, with all its uncertainties and unexpected twists and turns, or simply the way things fail to turn out how we had expected or secretly dreamed, can prove to be the source of disillusionment and discouragement to an extent we could never have imagined in our earlier days of blissful naivety. Life's seemingly random roller coaster can hurl the strongest saint out of their familiar world of happiness and certainty into one of perplexity and panic. It is perhaps the most unsettling, disturbing place in which to be. Even God's mighty prophet Elijah knew what it was to become discouraged by life's unpredictable character. After challenging and shaming the 450 prophets of Baal on Mount Carmel, seeing the fire of God fall and receiving such heavenly vindication, he, no doubt, expected that wicked King Ahab and Queen Jezebel would repent, put God first, and the nation would be brought back to God. But no such thing happened. Ahab and Jezebel were as stubborn and hard-hearted as before, and the nation remained the same. Elijah felt discouraged, exhausted and afraid, told himself that his entire life and ministry were a miserable failure, and, in panic, fled for his life from the woman he had thought would be begging for forgiveness (1 Kings 19).

Skewed view of success

Most of us know something of this. Despite our best acts of faith and devotion, and our persistent and fervent prayers, things just don't turn out in life the way we'd hoped they would. We then presume that something has gone wrong or that we have failed in some way. The ice-thrower in such circumstances can be ourselves, and we can be pretty good at it, too. Whether it be a faulty theology we have embraced, a skewed view of God, ministry or 'success', or a variety of other defective expectations, we feel devastated. Having written the script for our lives, we feel disappointed that God seems either not to have read it, or worse, to have discarded it. Some of us set out, sure that we have been sent forth with an earth-shaking ministry—and surely it's good to have high expectations—yet time has proved that God has other plans. And we can be in no doubt that those plans are infinitely superior to ours. Scottish Bible teacher and writer *Oswald Chambers* (1874–1917) undoubtedly spoke from experience when he wrote, 'We have the idea that God is going to do some exceptional thing, that he is preparing and equipping us for some extraordinary work in the future. But as we grow in grace, we find that God is glorifying Himself here and now, in the present moment.'[25]

Flourishing where we are planted

In their poignant and disarmingly honest book, *Andrew and Rachel Wilson* share the struggles of raising two young children with special needs. Both speak about the godly, fiery ambitions they had in their younger days, as they envisaged their lives sacrificially laid down in God's service. Fuelled by the lives of past men and women of faith, Rachel imagined herself rescuing those trapped in the sex trade or caring for African orphans. For Andrew, a sharp-minded theologian and gifted communicator, a high-profile itinerant ministry seemed to be beckoning. But then life seemed to hurl a curveball as two children were born to them with severe autism, and their world was turned on its head. Their story is one of immense encouragement for us in recognizing that, firstly, God's ways are not our ways, and, secondly, glorifying God in the situation in which He has placed us is the highest of all callings.[26] Each and every Christian has a call upon their life. In one sense we have all been called to 'full-time service' and to be on the 'front line' in the battle. It is just a matter of recognizing where your front line is: whether it be in the home, place of study or work, or even upon a bed of sickness, serving our Lord Jesus with faith and faithfulness day after day, ignoring inner dreams of public applause and recognition. It is this that delivers us from frustration or overwhelming feelings of hopelessness, and allows us to see that, even in 'this' (our present circumstances), we are 'more than conquerors' and will one day hear our Saviour say to us before an assembled multitude, 'Well done, good and faithful servant!' (Rom. 8:37; Matt. 25:23).

FALLEN LEADERS

You were brought to Christ under his ministry. Since that day, he has held a special place in your affections—in fact, you feel an eternal indebtedness to him. You have looked up to him as the model Christian in his life and service for the Lord. And then the gut-wrenching news breaks that for some time he has been living a double life. The weeks pass, and the sordid details you just don't want to believe begin to unfold. Your stomach churns and your mind struggles to process the unsavoury revelations, yet strangely, no matter how repugnant the particulars are, it is the sense of bitter disappointment and betrayal that causes the deepest pain and brings the heaviest shower of ice upon your world.

This, tragically, is a scenario that many can identify with, and Satan achieves a great victory when he brings about the demise and shaming of a man who holds a high profile in the church or in the wider Christian world.

ICE AND FIRE

The best of men . . .

When a leader fails it is not only a grievous offence to God and to his people, but it also has the potential for widespread spiritual harm too terrifying to consider. Who can estimate how many followers of Christ, even if they have not stopped running the race, have been left with deep-rooted distrust or cynicism regarding the church after such a fall? At such a time, it is all too easy for those who profess to be believers to join hands with the enemies of Christ and the gospel in their cynical opinion that the church is a place for hypocrites, and that 'outsiders' live better lives without 'religion'.

It is right here that we must curtail the enemy's activity by fixing our eyes upon the pure and perfect Head, Jesus Christ, and by confidently pointing others to Him. The old maxim is still sound, 'The best of men are men at best', and it is no less true of Christian leaders. Whilst seeking always to honour them and submit joyfully to their authority (Heb. 13:17), we need to be realistic enough to recognize that no matter how filled with grace these saints are, they, like us all, are still sinful human beings with the propensity to commit even the gravest of sins.

Moving on

When such a calamity befalls us, what can we do?

- *Pray for the fallen one*—and, of course, for his or her family, who, above us all, will be in the direst position, struggling not only with the betrayal but also with having to cope with shame and distress on a scale we cannot begin to imagine. (Discipline and restoration

ICE AND FIRE

will inevitably need to be tackled by church leaders, so pray for them too.)

- *Look to Jesus*. He is the only perfect leader. And He will never betray or disappoint us (Heb. 12:2–3).

- *Protect yourself from cynicism*. Christ loves the church—she is His beloved bride—and although at times we may grieve over the sin within her (which we, of course, contribute to), He will, one day, 'present her to himself as a radiant church, without stain or wrinkle or any other blemish, but holy and blameless' (Eph. 5:27).

- *Forgive realistically*. We most likely are never going to forget the pain and betrayal, but we can and must pray (1) that we will have grace to forgive the fallen one from the heart; and (2) that he or she might experience that 'Godly sorrow [that] brings repentance that leads to salvation and leaves no regret' (2 Cor. 7:10).

- *Search yourself*. We can use such painful times as a precious opportunity to humble ourselves, increasing our determination to fight sin and renewing our determination to 'finish well'.

The reality is that leaders come and go, but Christ is the Chief Shepherd, and He will remain the faithful and true leader of His sheep.

OUR GREATEST ENEMY

If we are to avoid discouragement's vast battlefield of gaping pits, then we dare not neglect taking care of how we walk. Writing to young Timothy, Paul warns, 'Watch your life and doctrine closely. Persevere in them, because if you do, you will save both yourself and your hearers' (1 Tim. 4:16). Evangelist *John Wesley* confessed, 'Worst of all my foes, I fear the enemy within.'[27] We find it relatively easy to spot sins and weaknesses in others, but we often don't have the stomach to deal with our own. But the enemy of our souls knows each of us only too well, and knows exactly where our weaknesses are. *Thomas Brooks*, speaking of Satan as a master angler, writes, 'Satan's first device to draw the soul into sin is, to present the bait—and hide the hook.'[28]

Know yourself

We need to know ourselves: our strengths, weaknesses, personality and moods. For example, if you are a passionate person, the devil will tempt you along the line of lust. If you are mellow and laid-back, then the temptation will be to lethargy and carelessness. If conscientious, he will make you a workaholic, busy in the kingdom but perhaps neglecting the King. If struggling financially, he will tempt you to bitterness and feelings of defeat. If prospering, then he will tempt you to presumption and prayerlessness. If you have a tender conscience, you will be tempted to legalism and bondage; if you are among 'the strong', you will be tempted to take liberties that may lead to shipwrecking your faith. We may think that could never happen to us, but that is yet another of his snares. Brooks alarms us with the awful potential just one sin has to harm. One sin barred Adam from the Garden, God, *life*! We must remember that one sin brought death to Achan and his entire family. One sin will grieve the Holy Spirit. One sin makes the heart harder, the conscience deader. One sin can carry a person to hell for ever. 'For whoever keeps the whole law and yet stumbles at just one point is guilty of breaking all of it,' writes James (James 2:10).

TEN SPECIAL HELPS

Pastor and popular blogger *Tim Challies* helpfully paraphrases Brooks's 'Conclusion', where the Puritan provides us with 'Ten Special Helps against Satan's Devices':[29]

1. *Be Ruled by the Word.* Make the Word of God your rule and authority and live in obedience to all it says . . .

2. *Beware of Grieving the Holy Spirit.* It is the Holy Spirit who gives the Christian the ability to discern Satan's temptations and to see his hand in and behind life's circumstances . . .

3. *Labor for Wisdom.* There is a great difference between knowledge and wisdom . . .

4. *Resist the First Stirring of Temptation.* It is safe to resist temptation and dangerous to dabble in it. 'He that will play with Satan's bait, will quickly be taken with Satan's hook' . . .

5. *Labor to Be Filled with the Spirit* . . . When it comes to fighting Satan's temptations, it is better to have a heart filled with the Spirit than a head filled with facts.

6. *Keep Humble* . . . The humble person is neither drawn in by what Satan offers, nor terrified by his threats.

7. *Be Constantly on Guard* . . . Satan strengthens his assaults when the soul grows drowsy and careless. So be constantly on guard . . .

8. *Continue Communing with God* . . . 'A soul high in communion with God may be tempted, but will not easily be conquered' . . .

9. *Do Not Engage Satan in Your Own Strength.* You need to draw the power, and even the desire, to resist sin from Jesus Christ and you need to do this every day . . .

10. *Pray Constantly*. 'Prayer is a shelter to the soul, a sacrifice to God and a scourge to the devil.' So pray and pray constantly . . .

The prayer found at the end of Psalm 139 is one I often resort to in order to deal with my own slippery heart:

Search me, God, and know my heart;
   test me and know my anxious thoughts.
See if there is any offensive way in me,
   and lead me in the way everlasting. (vv. 23–24)

Looking to Christ

Reformer *John Wycliffe* reminds us that there can never be room for either complacency, on the one hand, or despondency, on the other: 'Let no man think himself to be holy because he is not tempted, for the holiest and highest in life have the most temptations. How much higher the hill is, so much is the wind there greater; so, how much higher the life is, so much the stronger is the temptation of.'[30] Saintly Scottish minister *Robert Murray M'Cheyne* (1813–1843) reminds us that we are never out of danger whilst in the body:

I am tempted to think that I am now an established Christian, that I have overcome this or that lust so long, that I have got into the habit of the opposite grace, so that there is no fear; I may venture very near the temptation, nearer than other men. This is a lie of Satan. One might as well speak of gunpowder getting by habit of resisting fire, so as not to catch spark. As long as powder is wet, it resists the spark; but when it becomes dry, it is ready to explode at the first touch. As long as the Spirit dwells in my heart, He deadens me to sin, so that, if lawfully called through temptation, I may reckon upon God carrying me through. But when the Spirit leaves me, I am like dry gunpowder. Oh for a sense of this![31]

ICE AND FIRE

M'Cheyne's godly biographer and close friend *Andrew Bonar* comments regarding his subject, 'It was his own inner persuasion that few had more to struggle with in the inner man. Who can tell what wars go on within?'[32] So, whilst being vigilant in guarding ourselves from the enemies around us, let us not neglect that which dwells within us. And, at all times, we dare not forget the grace of God that is able to keep us not only from falling, but from a lack of faith and expectancy in the kingdom, forgetting that God uses imperfect beings to accomplish His perfect plans. M'Cheyne helpfully advises, 'For every look at yourself, take ten looks at Christ.'[33]

The flawed need not be floored!

If I am brutally honest, my forty years of Christian living and service have been forty years of blunders, stupidity and, at times, outright sin. But if I reflect too much on this, my focus becomes totally skewed, and I am looking to myself rather than fixing my eyes upon the wonderful Saviour I serve, and His uniquely glorious ability to 'draw a straight line with a crooked stick', making something eternally valuable out of my mess. God is used to using flawed men and women to accomplish His eternal purposes. We see this clearly demonstrated in the lineage of the Messiah. Earthy American author *Ann Voskamp*, commenting on Matthew's genealogy (Matt. 1:1–16), writes, 'The coming of Christ was through messed up monarchs and battling brothers, through affairs and adulteries, feuds and skeletons in the cupboards . . . '[34] Whilst not wishing to cheapen God's grace, we do rest in it, and we rejoice that our failures need not disqualify us from pressing on to further usefulness in His service. When the

Accuser comes upon us like a flood—attempting to keep us away from the cleansing blood of Calvary and seeking with all his malicious cunning to leave us in the icy shadows of condemnation—let us never tire of reminding ourselves that *God* declares, 'There is now *no* condemnation for those who are in Christ Jesus' (Rom. 8:1). The Word of God is the sword of the Spirit, and we must constantly feed our minds with Scripture so that, like the Son of God, we can confidently repel each attack with 'It is written . . . ' (Matt. 4:1–11). We must constantly be aware that Satan's great work in the true child of God is to rob him or her of assurance, to steal away the joy of the Lord which is our strength. I may still be a sinner, but I can rejoice incessantly that I am a *forgiven* sinner!

Not far from New York, in a cemetery lone,
Close guarding its grave stands a simple headstone;
And on it the inscription is one word alone, FORGIVEN.

No sculptor's fine art has embellished its form,
But constantly there, through the rain and the storm,
It bears this lone word from a poor fallen worm, FORGIVEN.

It gives not the date of the silent one's birth,
Reveals not his frailties, nor lies of his worth,
But speaks out this word from his few feet of earth—FORGIVEN.

The death is unmentioned, the name is untold,
Beneath lies the body, corrupted and cold,
But above rests his spirit, at home in the fold; FORGIVEN!

(Author unknown)

NOTES OVERLEAF ➡

ICE AND FIRE

Notes

1 Percy Livingstone Parker (ed.), *The Journal of John Wesley* (Chicago: Moody, 1951), p. 169.

2 William Gurnall, *The Christian in Complete Armour*, Vol. 2 (Edinburgh: Banner of Truth, 1988), p. 274.

3 In John Blanchard, *Gathered Gold* (Darlington: Evangelical Press, 1984), p. 37.

4 *Five Pioneer Missionaries* (Edinburgh: Banner of Truth, 1987), p. 305.

5 'Charles Spurgeon', Bible.org, https://bible.org/illustration/charles-spurgeon-1.

6 For example, on Twitter, @timkellernyc, 29 October 2013.

7 A. W. Tozer, *The Pursuit of God* (London: Marshall, Morgan & Scott, 1963), p. 113.

8 Matthew Henry, *Commentary on the Whole Bible* (Edinburgh: Marshall, Morgan & Scott, 1960), on Numbers 12:2, p. 153.

9 John Blanchard, *Sifted Silver* (Darlington: Evangelical Press, 1995), p. 268.

10 C. S. Lewis, *The Four Loves* (New York: Harcourt, 1960), Kindle edn, loc. 1541.

11 Adolf Hitler, writing to Hermann Rauschning, quoted by Warren Wiersbe on 2 Kings 10–11, *Old Testament Commentary* (Colorado Springs: David C Cook, 2007), p. 696.

12 Medical Missionary News, December 2017.

13 D. M. Lloyd-Jones, *Studies in the Sermon on the Mount* (London: Inter-Varsity Press, 1976), p. 464.

14 Richard Collier, *The General Next to God* (London/Glasgow: Collins/Fontana, 1968), p. 220.

15 Wong Ming-Dao, *A Stone Made Smooth* (Southampton: Mayflower Christian Books, 1981), p. 213.

16 In Blanchard, *Gathered Gold*, p. 37.

17 J. C. Marshman, *The Life and Times of Carey, Marshman, and Ward*, 2 vols (London: Longman, Brown, Green, Longmans & Roberts, 1859), quoted at

'William Carey (Missionary)', Wikipedia, https://en.wikipedia.org/wiki/
William_Carey_(missionary).

18 William Gurnall, *The Christian in Complete Armour*, Vol. 1 (Edinburgh:
Banner of Truth Trust, 2017), p. 27.

19 'Taking Criticism', excerpt from Redeemer City to City Blog, 'How Do You
Take Criticism of Your Views?' by Tim Keller, Daily Keller, 25 June 2017,
http://dailykeller.com/page/9/.

20 Thomas à Kempis, *The Imitation of Christ*, trans. E. M. Blaiklock (London:
Hodder & Stoughton, 1987), Book 2, Chapter 6, paras 2, 3.

21 Andrew Murray, *Humility* (1895; Public domain; Kindle edn), Preface.

22 Name changed for confidentiality.

23 Name changed for confidentiality.

24 Name changed for confidentiality.

25 Oswald Chambers, *My Utmost for His Highest* (Uhrichsville, OH: Barbour
Publishing, 2014), 4 June.

26 Andrew and Rachel Wilson, *The Life You Never Expected* (Nottingham: Inter-
Varsity Press, 2015).

27 In Blanchard, *Gathered Gold*, p. 295.

28 Thomas Brooks, *Precious Remedies against Satan's Devices* (Edinburgh:
Banner of Truth, 1968), p. 29.

29 Based on ibid., p. 243. Tim Challies, '10 Ways to Resist the Devil', Challies.
com (blog), 18 July 2013, https://www.challies.com/reading-classics-
together/10-ways-to-resist-the-devil/.

30 John Wycliffe, *Writings of the Reverend and Learned John Wickliff* (London:
Religious Tract Society, 1831), p. 100.

31 Andrew Bonar, *Memoir and Remains of Rev. Robert Murray M'Cheyne*
(Edinburgh: Banner of Truth, 1978 repr.), p. 152.

32 Ibid., p. 143.

33 Ibid., p. 293.

34 Ann Voskamp, *The Greatest Gift: Unwrapping the Full Love Story of
Christmas* (Carol Stream, IL: Tyndale House, 2013), p. ix.

PART 2

FIRE

6 Fan into flame

Therefore I remind you to stir up the gift of God which is in you through the laying on of my hands. For God has not given us a spirit of fear, but of power and of love and of a sound mind. (2 Tim. 1:6–7 NKJV)

O God of burning altar fire,
O God of love's consuming flame,
Make pure the flame of our desire
To win the lost to seek Thy Name. (Amy Carmichael)

There can come, in life, those dark moments when we feel ourselves totally unfit for serving God in any capacity whatsoever. Perhaps we even reach the point of despair. We may have spent time in calm contemplation, considered the task before us, then turned and scrutinized our personal paltry gifts and resources. Our response is to keep our heads down and plan how we might creep to heaven with as few as possible discovering just how inept and blundering were our attempts at living the Christian life.

At such times, we can be sure of one thing: we have shifted our focus away from Christ and onto ourselves, and we are paying the just penalty for our foolishness and self-pity. But there is a flame God lights by the Holy Spirit in the hearts of men and women which, no matter how hard they may try, men and demons—even our own folly and unbelief—cannot extinguish.

NOT A SPIRIT OF FEAR

The apostle Paul, writing to a fearful young man,

encourages him with the words 'Therefore I remind you to stir up the gift of God which is in you through the laying on of my hands. For God has not given us a spirit of fear, but of power and of love and of a sound mind' (2 Tim. 1:6–7 NKJV). We may be neither apostles nor preachers, but when we are 'born from above', a holy fire is implanted in our souls that we dare not allow to be doused. In this dark and hopeless world, we are all called to be worshippers and witnesses of God. Whilst Paul is referring to a spiritual gift entrusted to Timothy for which he is responsible as a pastor and teacher, the wider application must not be avoided. God has entrusted the gospel to every Christian and to every local church, and has given gifts to every child of God, that we might be the people we should be in our generation. We have been charged to preserve the gospel, to live the gospel, to preach the gospel, and to be faithful in holding out this 'lifeline' from God to man. We have been commissioned to take it to the four corners of the earth, so that every person may hear and respond to the good news.

But who really is up to such a daunting duty—apart from a gracious provision from above! There has to be a holy flame within our hearts. Bible commentator *Matthew Poole* quaintly drives home our responsibility in keeping this flame burning: 'Paul, writing to Timothy, adviseth him to put new life unto that holy fire—the word signifies the recovering of fire choked with ashes or decaying—which God had kindled in him.'[1]

STRANGE FIRE?
At this point our theological radar may kick in to alert us

to excess or even heresy at the very mention of that phrase 'holy fire'—and we must painfully confess that the beautiful biblical symbol of the Holy Spirit as fire has often been woefully misused and abused. So inclined are we to illusions, delusions and even fantasies, it is right always to be vigilant. But let us not allow such an essential biblical truth to be hijacked, denying us access to this vital source of blessing. Our enemy knows only too well how much we need the real thing. Genuine Holy Spirit fire is what is desperately needed in these days, so it is no surprise that such fierce battles exist among the Lord's people in this area.

FIRE SIGNIFICANT

When a small flame rested upon each disciple's head on that unique Pentecost day, it was beautifully symbolic and significant. The outpouring of the Holy Spirit in extraordinary power was to show that God would equip weak and fearful men and women with a heavenly stimulus for worldwide witness for all generations. Pastor and theologian *James Montgomery Boice* has a chapter in his commentary on Acts entitled 'The Incendiary Fellowship' to describe the character and nature of the early Christians. They were those who, having themselves been 'set ablaze', were able to set others ablaze.[2]

Speaking on the symbolism of fire, *C. H. Spurgeon* said,

Fire does more than give light; it inflames; and the flames which sat upon each showed them that they were to be ablaze with love, intense zeal, burning with self-sacrifice; and that they were to go forth among men to speak not with the chill tongue of deliberate logic, but with burning tongues of passionate pleading; persuading and entreating men to come to Christ that they might live.[3]

The church began with fire and spread rapidly with that fire, and our world will not be impacted today without His followers being imbued with that same Holy Spirit fire. Not preachers only, but men and women indwelt by Jesus who, before ascending into heaven, promised that He would send One who not only would be with them, but who would actually dwell within them (John 14:17), and whose presence and power would enable them to live heavenly lives in a hellish world. The church dare not neglect this emphasis in its doctrine of pneumatology. No matter how slick our presentation or how adept we are at dodging bullets aimed at the church and its message, we need to be utterly convinced in the depth of our beings that God meant it when he said that it is 'Not by might nor by power, but by my Spirit . . . ' (Zech. 4:6). If this is true, it should not surprise us that men and demons will most certainly combine—using any and every means—to douse that necessary Flame which alone will enable the gospel to blaze and spread to every creature on the earth, despite every obstacle placed in our path.

GOD'S TREASURE IN EARTHEN VESSELS

Let us beware of consigning this emphasis of Holy Spirit fire to the garbage bin labelled 'fanaticism'—or, if we acknowledge it, of perhaps seeing it as relevant only for those called to some kind of 'upfront' ministry. Not at all. He was sent to empower those who genuinely take to heart the words of Jesus, 'apart from me you can do nothing'

(John 15:5). The Holy Spirit is God's gracious provision for those who have tried their best and failed! God delights in coming to those of us who have realized that without His constant supply of grace and power we are totally useless at living the Christian life.

Reflect on these words written to her pastor by a desperate yet refreshingly honest woman:

I am the world's number one failure. My marriage is failing, I seem to do everything wrong in raising my children. I'm not even able to understand the Bible very well, most of it is over my head. I feel as if I am not worth anything to anyone. I've not been a very good wife, mother or Christian. I have to be the world's greatest failure.[4]

The pastor rejoiced to receive the letter, because he knew that there is always hope for such a person. Only the sick need a doctor. Only the weak need strength. Only the foolish need wisdom. Only the cold need heat. Only the empty need filling. And this, of course, is God's way: the guilty coming for pardon, the sorrowing for joy, the impure for purity, the lost for direction, the weak for power. The goal, of course, is that we might then be what God wants us to be, and do what God wants us to do. It is this kind of relationship which produces a grateful, joyful dependency. As an old revival hymn movingly expresses it:

I praise Thee, Lord, for cleansing me from sin;
Fulfil Thy word and make me pure within.
Fill me with fire where once I burned with shame;
Grant my desire to magnify Thy name.
(J. Edwin Orr, 'Search Me, O God, and Know My Heart Today')

ICE AND FIRE

A SUPERIOR LOVE

I was converted to Christ dramatically from a life of addiction. In a split second I was released from alcohol's unyielding grip which had bound me for years. One taste of heaven's joys and I knew instantly that this was the thing I had really thirsted for all those years. There is no medical cure for alcoholism, but this was what *Thomas Chalmers*, a Scottish minister and theologian centuries before, described as 'The expulsive power of a new affection'.[5] His thesis, in a nutshell, was that reasoning and willpower are never successful in delivering us from the powers of this world that grip and enthral us. The only way to dispossess our hearts of an old affection or love is by the expulsive power of a new or higher one. That was certainly true in my case. No amount of reasoning, threatening or tearful pleading from my long-suffering wife had any effect—even though I knew she was right. Common sense, wrecked cars, my declining health—and virtually everybody else—were all on her side. The problem *always* is that the controlling powers over a sinner are just too great. *But* . . . whenever heaven invades earth, and a feeble human being is melted by a 'sight' of the overwhelming love of Jesus, it is 'game over' for sin's captivity. The Holy Spirit alone can accomplish this work; it was for this reason He was sent. When He reveals Christ to the imprisoned soul, the captive is released and worship is spontaneous—it is the rejoicing, reasonable response of a guilty sinner who breathlessly grasps that he is loved and even indwelt by the King of kings, and all out of sheer astonishing grace. The God who moments before was justly angry with me has suddenly, somehow, become my closest friend. *Jarrod Cooper* expresses this well:

King of kings, majesty,
God of Heaven living in me,
gentle Saviour, closest friend,
strong deliverer, beginning and end,
all within me falls at your throne.

Your majesty, I can but bow,
I lay my all before you now.
In royal robes I don't deserve
I live to serve your majesty.

God of heaven living in me! It is the expulsive power of a new nature—a love for one thing displaced by a superior love. Thomas Chalmers was applying his principle primarily to Christians overpowered by sin and enchanted by this world's temptations. But, surely, the same liberating power is available for believers who simply feel knocked down and defeated by life itself and a multitude of things that threaten to overwhelm us. When we feel buried under a mountain of ice that the powers behind this fallen world have thrown at us, we can be visited by our God and be filled time and time again with heavenly fire. Isn't this why Paul in Ephesians commands us to 'be [continually] filled with the Spirit' (Eph. 5:18)? This injunction is given to believers in the midst of teaching on how to live in the home and in the workplace, and, at that, in a world of debauchery and rebellion against God. Being filled with the Holy Spirit is not an option, but a necessity.

A 'NICE FEELING'?

Not very often. Although we are thankful for every 'foretaste of glory divine'—a shaft of joy that we receive on occasion—

we are talking ultimately about God's provision of grace in order to be overcomers in a world that causes us to want to throw in the towel on a daily basis. When Paul prays for the church, he prays that they may have 'power', *not* in order to boast of experiences, but that in realizing how loved they are by Christ, they might survive the worst of ordeals that will come their way (Eph. 3:16–21). I doubt very much if Andrew and Rachel Wilson (see previous chapter) experience 'spiritual highs' when sleep-deprived and care-worn in raising their severely autistic children. But they are able to continue with incredible love, passion and perseverance because of the Spirit's power and presence in their lives. Believers who are persecuted and even tortured for their faith and faithfulness—at this very moment—are able to continue for that same reason. I doubt that those locked away, half-starved in a North Korean camp, or Christians placed in scorching-hot shipping containers in Eritrea for years on end, are in ecstasies of delight as they suffer so courageously for following the One who loved them and died for them.

A GRACIOUS PROVISION

So every provision has been made for those who have committed themselves to taking up their cross and following Jesus. Let us look, not at the rapidly enveloping darkness, but rather with hope-filled expectancy to the supernatural provision God has promised us, through the Holy Spirit. But for our part, we are called to 'fan into flame' that which perhaps has begun to burn low. *William Booth*, addressing a group of young Salvation Army officers, said (or perhaps barked!), 'I want you young men always to bear in mind that it is the nature of fire to go out; you must keep it stirred and fed, and the ashes removed.'[6]

NOTES OVERLEAF ➡

Notes

1 Matthew Poole, *A Commentary on the Whole Bible*, Vol. 3, *Matthew–Revelation* (Mclean, VA: Macdonald Publishing Co., 1985), p. 791.

2 James Montgomery Boice, *Acts* (Grand Rapids: Baker, 1997), p. 45.

3 C. H. Spurgeon, 'The Pentecostal Wind and Fire', Sermon on Acts 2:2–4, in *Wind and Fire: Ten Sermons on the Holy Spirit* (Belfast: Ambassador, 1995), p. 95.

4 In David Wilkerson, *Have You Felt Like Giving Up Lately?* (Grand Rapids: Spire, 2015), p. 121.

5 Thomas Chalmers (1780–1847) was a Scottish minister, professor of theology and leader of the Free Church of Scotland.

6 Quoted by Warren Wiersbe, *The Wiersbe Bible Commentary: Old Testament* (Colorado Springs: David C Cook, 2007), commenting on start of Neh. 13, p. 788.

7 Fire-carriers

John was a lamp that burned and gave light. (John 5:35)

For the keepers of the flame of hope,
The fire of love, the spark of the beauty way,
The eternal blaze of truth.
Fire Carrier, burn once again, burn once again.
('Fire Carrier', by Murray Kyle)

'Am I ignitable?' (Jim Elliot)

Our world is in deep, dire, desperate darkness. The need of the hour is for 'fire-carriers': those who, despite the fire-quenching attitudes, atmosphere and antipathy of our world, have a burning desire to see the gospel of Jesus Christ spread so that 'the earth will be filled with the knowledge of the glory of the LORD as the waters cover the sea' (Hab. 2:14). It is, therefore, essential that everyone who claims to be a follower of Jesus Christ has a world-conquering vision and passion burning within. In order to help and inspire us in this, we will, in the remainder of this book, seek encouragement from 'fire-carriers' of past days. Some are celebrated 'heroes', while others are little known in our day, but their status in the church or in history is irrelevant. We look to the past, not out of life-sapping spiritual nostalgia, nor because we are unable to recognize that God is at work and using men and women in our own day (in fact, not all our subjects are dead!); it is simply because we trace the hand of God in a special way upon certain people, some who 'by faith, still [speak], even though . . . dead' (Heb. 11:4). These are men and women of holy fire who by faith 'conquered kingdoms' and 'whose weakness was turned to strength' as they surrendered their meagre resources to the Omnipotent God (Heb. 11:33–34). In these days of increasing pressure, we stand in constant need of motivation and to be reminded that we are on a mission, and that no matter how difficult the times in which we live, our mighty God can take and use any one of us.

CHRISTIAN BIOGRAPHY

For me, almost from that first glorious day when I tasted the love of Christ, I was enthralled by two wonderful things: the Scriptures and Christian biography. As a rookie Christian, I began to read how God had used all kinds of men and women to work out His plans and purposes. I was thrilled and fascinated by the sheer variety of people God used. Different ages, personalities, theological convictions—but one wonderful common denominator: a passion for the glory of God. My natural response was, 'If God can use them, then why not me?' *John Piper*, in encouraging pastors to read biographies and to encourage their churches to do the same, says, 'We are supposed to inspire people with great possibilities. Not that God can't give vision, direction and inspiration. But He also uses human agents to stir up his people.' He argues that to help us 'run with perseverance the race marked out for us' (Heb. 12:1) we can be inspired by those who ran before, hence the catalogue provided in the eleventh chapter of Hebrews. Commending the use and relevance of biography, Piper continues, 'Christian biography is the means by which "body life" cuts across the generations.'[1]

I personally am indebted to many people over the years for their godly lives and examples, but the majority of them, by far, are dead. When at Bible college in South Wales many years ago, I would often escape the hubbub of student life by slipping out to a small lecture room in which all the Christian biographies were kept. I would sit, basking in the atmosphere of that fragrant sacred space, alone with my 'friends'. Although separated by many centuries in some cases, they were a present encouragement as I felt the same heavenly pressure to serve the same Saviour in the same glorious work as they. God has so placed us in these days that we have that vast 'cloud of witnesses' (Heb. 12:1) who have run their race, but who continue to urge you and me on to heroic efforts for Jesus. In order that we might be better equipped to be *fire-carriers* in our generation, we will look at men and women whom we in the modern church stand in danger of forgetting—and whose legacy is far too precious for us to lose. But whether they are those we have heard of already or those whose names and lives never made the 'Top 100', it really doesn't matter. In fact, in some areas I have sought deliberately to avoid the more obvious choice of 'hero'.

THE FIRE IMAGERY

First, though, it might encourage us to be reminded how the imagery of fire, flame and phrases like 'burning passion' have inspired others through the years. Of course, our God is a consuming fire; He burns with holy love and holy anger. It follows, then, that there should be something fire-like about those who claim to be indwelt by Him. *Amy Carmichael*, whose passionate love was poured out in India rescuing little girls from a life of abuse, prayed for herself:

Give me the love that leads the way,
The faith that nothing can dismay,
The hope no disappointments tire,
The passion that will burn like fire;
Let me not sink to be a clod;
Make me Thy fuel, O flame of God

God is seen as One who is aflame; the gospel is a message that is aflame. Significantly, *Michael Reeves*, writing about the Reformation, a time in history when God broke mightily into Europe's darkness, entitled his book *The Unquenchable Flame*. The emphasis is never upon ourselves, but on the God who, even though our faith be reduced to dying embers, can come with a breath from heaven and set us ablaze. Amy Carmichael, however, pointed out that the flame needs fuel when she prayed earnestly, 'Make me Thy fuel, O flame of God.' Not very many years after, *Jim Elliot*, who was to pay the ultimate price, laying down his life in pioneering gospel work at the age of twenty-eight, was inspired by Amy Carmichael's words and challenged himself, writing in his diary, 'Am I ignitable?' It would seem that those closest to God will burn in some way with His holy love and passion.

THE BURNING ONES

In Isaiah 6 we read of awesome heavenly beings called 'seraphs', or 'seraphim'. This is the only scriptural reference to them, and the word means, literally, 'the burning ones'. They do not appear in the form of men as do other angels recorded in Scripture, and though, like the cherubim, they are depicted as having wings, they appear to be a different, even higher order of angelic creatures. In the context of Isaiah, the seraphim are connected with proximity to God's throne and His utter holiness. They are standing and serving before the throne, awaiting His commands. Isaiah tells us that seraphim were in attendance above him, and each had six wings: with two they covered their faces, with two they covered their feet and with two they flew. Regarding their ministering in the presence of God, the greatly missed American theologian *R. C. Sproul* commented, 'The *seraphim* who worship Him in heaven have never sinned; nevertheless, they cannot look on God directly. They must protect their eyes from a direct apprehension of the Lord's transcendent purity or they will be blinded by the light of His majestic glory.'[2] They are fiery servants of the God of fire. Similarly, despite all the earthly passions and longings that raged within a hot-blooded male, young Jim Elliot was not content merely to be challenged by Amy Carmichael's life, but took her words for his own personal prayer of commitment, crying unreservedly, 'Make *me* Thy fuel, O flame of God.'

DEAD, BUT STILL SPEAKING

It is significant to note how biography encouraged and impacted this young man. Again, reading his diary, we see what was happening in the depths of his soul, even whilst at university:

I see the value of Christian biography tonight as I have been reading David Brainerd's 'Diary' much today. It stirs me up much to pray and wonder at my nonchalance while I have not power from God. I have considered Hebrews 13:7 just now, regarding the remembrance of certain ones who spoke the word of God, 'Consider the outcome of their life, and imitate their faith.' I recall now the challenge of [Jonathan] Goforth's 'Life' and 'By My Spirit', read in the summer of 1947, the encouragement of Hudson Taylor's 'Spiritual Secret', and 'The Growth of a Soul'. There are incidents which instruct me now from the reading of J. G. Paton's biography I read last winter. And now this fresh Spirit-quickened history of Brainerd. O Lord, let me be granted grace to 'imitate their faith'.

Hot on the heels of this diary entry comes perhaps the most quoted of all missionary quotes: 'He is no fool who gives what he cannot keep, to gain what he cannot lose.' The context is noteworthy: the reading, challenge and deep encouragement of Christian biography![3]

ICE AND FIRE

Our aim now will be to take note of the lives of various saints, most of whom have run their race. We will especially note how they coped with setbacks and discouragement—not that we might be left standing in jaw-dropped awe of them, although that might well be the result; nor that we should feel pressed to enter the ministry or be called to missionary service—although that would be great. Rather, the outcome will hopefully be simply to see in these vignettes—mere snippets taken from their life stories—how flesh-and-blood mortals just like us, with the same God, can triumph in times of trial, pressure and heartbreak, so that we ourselves, when ice-covered, downcast and despondent, might receive heaven's fire to strengthen us for the battle in which we are engaged in our day on our own particular 'front line'.

Notes

1 John Piper, 'Brothers, Read Christian Biography', Desiring God, 1 January 1995, https://www.desiringgod.org/articles/brothers-read-christian-biography.

2 'Seraphim Viewing the Lord', Ligonier Ministries, https://www.ligonier.org/learn/devotionals/seraphim-viewing-lord/.

3 Elisabeth Elliot, *Shadow of the Almighty* (Bromley: STL, 1979), p. 110.

8 Keepers of the flame

Then I said, 'I will not make mention of Him,
Nor speak anymore in His name.'
But His word was in my heart like a burning fire
Shut up in my bones;
I was weary of holding it back,
And I could not. (Jer. 20:9 NKJV)

All God's giants have been weak men who did great things for
God because they reckoned on God being with them. (James
Hudson Taylor)

Never are we to entertain the thought that the darkness of the days in which we live is unusual, nor think that, perhaps, had we have lived in a different era, living for Christ would have been easier. With a healthy realism, John the apostle wrote that 'the whole world is under the control of the evil one', but not before encouraging his readers that 'everyone born of God overcomes the world. This is the victory that has overcome the world, even our faith' (1 John 5:19, 4). In every generation there have been those saints who have shone like beacons, but they would be the first to say that it was not of them, but was God working in and through them. And they would be right. If that were not the case, what you are about to read would become just another batch of ice hurled at you. The qualities we see displayed in the following saints of God are simply the fruit of lives lived in total dependence upon

Jehovah Jireh, the One able to meet *all* your needs 'according to the riches of his glory in Christ Jesus' (Phil. 4:19).

ORDINARY, YET REMARKABLE

In the following pages we will see ordinary men and women with total reliance upon the Holy Spirit to do that which they could not do in themselves. And He is able to do the same for us; whether He comes to us like a mighty rushing wind or as a gentle summer breeze, the outcome is the same: people living above their own ability. In order that we might be kept from lives of spiritual lethargy or fearfulness, may we too receive grace to 'imitate those who through faith and patience inherit what has been promised' (Heb. 6:12). And we can do no better than start by considering the life of the poor self-educated cobbler from Northampton, who against all the odds was eventually hailed as 'The father of modern mission'.

FAITH: WILLIAM CAREY,
THE PERSEVERING PLODDER
(1761–1834)

The young man in an ill-fitting wig stood before the august assembly of ministers and preached his heart out. 'Multitudes in "heathen" lands remain in utter darkness without the gospel, and no one seems concerned,' was the thrust of his impassioned plea. He felt he had given it his best shot, taking as his text Isaiah 54:2–3: 'Lengthen thy cords, and strengthen thy stakes; for thou shalt break forth on the right hand and on the left; and thy seed shall inherit the Gentiles, and make the desolate cities to be inhabited' (KJV). His message was punchy, divided under two main headings: expect great things from God, and attempt great things for God.

When he had finished, he sat down, his emotions poured out, his energy spent, with that vulnerability only preachers know after having given their all. Painful memories shot into William Carey's mind of a stinging public rebuke given him at an earlier meeting. A senior minister, John Ryland, had scolded him with what must now be the most famous of all Christian put-downs: 'Young man, sit down; when God is pleased to convert the heathen world, He will do it without your help or mine.' Carey had been impressed by the zeal of early Moravian missionaries, and increasingly dismayed at his fellow Protestants' lack of missions interest. But he had tried once more, and now he waited nervously for the response.

However, caution seemed to reign, and the leaders—whose evangelistic fervour was undoubtedly quenched by a prevailing hyper-Calvinism—were negative, bound by the same doubts and indifference that had thwarted his previous efforts. In agony of distress, the young minister grabbed the arm of the highly respected Andrew Fuller and cried, 'Is there nothing again going to be done, sir?' The Holy Spirit clothed his intense words with power, and Fuller trembled as the heartbroken plea 'stabbed his soul awake'. This was to be not only the turning point in the life of Fuller (who later compared the sending of William Carey to India to lowering him into a deep gold mine), but also a moment that would change the face of world missions, bringing eternal blessing to untold millions. In October 1792, the Baptist Missionary Society was formed, and within a year, Carey—their first missionary—was on a ship bound for India.

From little acorns . . .

Born on 17 August 1761 in the rural village of Paulerspury in Northamptonshire, England's most central county, William was the eldest of five children born to humble weavers Edmund and Elizabeth Carey. His childhood was a happy one and he showed a keen interest in the natural sciences—botany in particular—and possessed a natural gift for languages—all of which was to play its part in his later life. At the age of fourteen, he was apprenticed by his father to a local shoemaker, and at this time he came under the influence of a fellow apprentice, John Warr, who was an unashamed Dissenter. As a nominal Church of England attendee, William despised the Dissenters, yet he became both convicted and drawn by the reality of the other lad's faith, eventually leaving his church to join with the Nonconformists. Although he was unsure of the exact date of his conversion, Carey must have been around eighteen years old. His spiritual awakening seemed to cause him to widen his horizons, being stirred to the need of missions through reading *The Last Voyage of Captain Cook*. This adventure gripped his soul.

Care for soles to concern for souls

His mind also was stimulated, and he began learning Latin, Greek, Hebrew and Italian, and started out as a lay preacher. It is no wonder that his humble cottage became known as 'Carey's College'. He met and married Dorothy ('Dolly') Plackett, who soon gave birth to their first child, a daughter, Ann. However, life for this young family was not easy; financial struggles were one trial to cope with, but they faced a greater, heartbreaking trial when their daughter died following a fever in her second year. Because his was a poorly paid profession, the Careys began to sink into poverty. But, as time passed, the cobbler's caring for soles was being overshadowed by his growing concern for human souls. Though preaching regularly in the locality and now working as a schoolmaster, he was burdened by the fact that a world was perishing without knowledge of the only Saviour. It was said of him, 'The map of the world hung in Carey's work room; but it only hung on the wall because it already hung in his heart.' In 1789, he was called to be the full-time pastor of Harvey Lane Baptist Church in Leicester, and after his probationary period he was ordained as a Baptist minister in May 1791.

First years in India

With conflicts with the Baptist hierarchy now behind him and the Baptist Missionary Society freshly formed, the pioneer and his family set sail for India on 13 June 1793, accompanied by John Thomas, a former surgeon, with his wife and daughter. Many battles were still to be fought, of course—with the British East India shipping company, for one, who refused to transport the unwelcome missionaries. But, after change of ship and various other traumas en route, the band eventually arrived in India on 10 November after an eventful five-month voyage, during which Carey reportedly threw overboard the wig he had worn since losing most of his hair prematurely in his early twenties. No doubt, he reasoned that image would be the very least of his concerns. Unable to stay in Calcutta (Kolkata), the missionaries moved thirty miles north, to the Portuguese settlement of Bandel, but it was not long before they were opposed once more, this time by the anti-missionary attitude of the British Colonial Government. Finances also looked to being a major problem, and so, seeking to be self-supporting, the missionaries moved north to Midnapore, where Carey, out of necessity, managed an indigo plant owned by a friend of John Thomas, whilst learning the Bengali language.

Struggles

During those first seven years, he completed the first edition of his Bengali New Testament, all the while creating the principles on which a community of missionaries could be formed and supported. But those early years were a time of enormous discouragement for Carey: his wife's tragic descent into insanity, not one convert seen, and then struggles with illness and debt. One can only imagine the taunts of the evil one, the feelings of self-doubt, and perhaps even the temptation to return home. At one particular low point he wrote, 'All of my friends are but One; I rejoice, however, that He is all-sufficient.' How different history might have looked had he succumbed. But he was made of sterner stuff, and refused to surrender to discouragement's weakening powers. And never should we overlook the fact that he was a man of prayer—earnest, persevering, faith-filled prayer. 'Prayer,' he said, 'secret, fervent, believing prayer lies at the root of all personal godliness.' In December 1800, having moved to Serampore (a Danish settlement where the British Government could not touch them), Carey baptized his first convert, Krishna Pal—after seven years of seemingly fruitless labour—and two months later published his first Bengali New Testament.

The plodder

In later years, Carey would say, 'I can plod, I can persevere to any definite pursuit. To this I owe everything.' He was a realistic man and possessed wisdom as well as patience, and realized that until the Scriptures were translated, published and circulated, progress would inevitably be slow. 'We have been breaking up the ground, rooting out the rank and most poisonous weeds, and sowing the good seed. Only a little return as yet appears, but the wise husbandman waits for the precious fruit of the earth, and has long patience over it.' This is not to say that he was free from the 'faith versus unbelief' battle we all face daily. Carey confesses he was 'often almost dried up by discouragement, and was tempted to go about his work like a soldier expecting defeat'. Then, on a 'good' day, he wrote in a letter, 'I have no doubt but God will establish His name in this country. Our labours may be only those of pioneers, but Truth will certainly prevail, and this kingdom amongst others will see the salvation of God.'

Ministry is always a team effort, and Carey was blessed to have been joined in his work by two gifted and able colleagues, Joshua Marshman and William Ward. Together, their accomplishments would go down in the annals of missions and church history as those of 'The Serampore Trio'.

Fiery trials

It is a stubborn fact that there is rarely progress in the gospel without suffering, trial and testing. On 12 March 1812, Carey was startled by the distress written across the face of Marshman when he unexpectedly burst into his Calcutta home. They had already been through a series of sorrows and trials of late; what further woe could there be? Marshman broke the catastrophic news to him that a fire had broken out in the mission printing works, which had been left a mere shell of burnt and bare walls. Worst of all, beside the destruction of the printing presses and metal print fonts of numerous languages and dialects, precious manuscripts, Bibles and dictionaries had perished; nothing had survived the furnace—'the labours of years consumed,' Carey later told a friend. The Job-like final blow came when an Indian, referring to the recent death of a second missionary colleague, asked, 'If God really sent you out to preach to us, why are two of you dead already?' When informed of the fire, however, Carey showed no sign of despair or even annoyance; instead he knelt and thanked God that he still had the strength and will to commence the work all over again. He began straight away, not wasting one moment in apportioning blame or indulging in self-pity. 'The Lord has laid me low,' he said, 'that I may look more simply to Him.'

What was achieved?

It is not only difficult, but actually impossible—and perhaps even dangerous—to seek to assess our labours for Christ and His kingdom. But it is worth noting a number of things achieved by Carey and his team. The whole Bible was translated into eight languages, the New Testament into twenty-seven languages, and portions of the Old Testament into ten other languages; dictionaries were compiled of Sanskrit, Marathi, Panjabi and Telugu (these are still respected today as authoritative); he started the still-influential Serampore College; they began churches and established nineteen mission stations; they formed one hundred rural schools encouraging the education of girls; they started the Horticultural Society of India; Carey served as a professor at Fort William College, Calcutta; he began the weekly publication *The Friend of India* (it continues today as *The Statesman*); they printed the first Indian newspaper; and they introduced the concept of the savings bank to assist poor farmers. He also fought against the burning of widows (*sati*) and helped lead to its ban in 1829.

The perspective of centuries

As noted, Carey testified modestly, 'I can plod,' but whilst acknowledging his humble testimony and recognizing that he was undoubtedly a man of dogged perseverance, it would be unwise not to balance that summary of his work and achievements with the assessments of two men serving Christ centuries later, who are in a position to view Carey with clearer perspective. *Dr Peter Masters*, the long-serving pastor of the Metropolitan Tabernacle in London, says of him, 'By the mighty power of God, Carey cut through formidable theological, legal and social prejudices of his day to become the most productive missionary church planter and Bible translator of all time.'[1] *John Piper* writes,

Carey was the morning star of modern missions. Between 1793 and 1865, a missionary movement never before seen in the history of the world reached virtually all the coastlands on earth. Then in 1865, Hudson Taylor founded the China Inland Mission, and from 1865 until 1934, another wave of missionary activity was released so that by 1974 virtually all the inlands—all the geographic countries of the world—were reached with the gospel.[2]

Death

On 9 June 1834, William Carey left this earth at the age of seventy-three, having never returned to England since leaving for India forty-one years previously. Not long before he died, he cautioned a friend, 'You have been saying much about Dr Carey and his work. When I am gone, say nothing about Dr Carey; speak about Dr Carey's Saviour.' He had requested that the following words of hymn-writer Isaac Watts be written on his tombstone:

A wretched, poor, and helpless worm,
On Thy kind arms I fall.

'These two lines and nothing more,' he insisted.

It is said that great men cast long shadows, and this was certainly true of William Carey. His influence is felt throughout the whole world to this day.

Gems

I'm not afraid of failure; I'm afraid of succeeding at things that don't matter.

What is there in the earth worth living for, but for the glory of God and the salvation of souls.

It is the duty of those who are entrusted with the Gospel to endeavour to make it known among all nations.

I will venture to go . . . but remember, you must hold the ropes.[3]

Love: Robert C. Chapman,
APOSTLE OF LOVE
(1803–1902)

If you have never heard of Robert Cleaver Chapman, this most self-effacing of men would have been delighted! Despite all his efforts to pass through this world unnoticed and unheralded, it simply was impossible for one who so radiated the love and grace of Jesus Christ. Many prominent Christian leaders of his day highly prized his fellowship and advice, among them George Müller, Hudson Taylor, J. C. Ryle and Charles Spurgeon ('The saintliest man I ever knew,' Spurgeon said of him). While he was noted for his kind, wise, gracious ways, his love shone above all, having the unique ability to bring harmony and reconciliation into the most difficult scenes of conflict in churches through his loving, irenic pastoral touch. It is no wonder he was often referred to as 'the apostle of love'. A well-known preacher who had hosted Chapman wrote to a friend in a letter, 'R. Chapman has just left us. He slept here last night, after preaching for me at John Street. Oh, what a man of God is he! What grace does he exhibit! Courage, meekness, self-denial, tenderness, perseverance, love for souls—all springing out of love of Christ and God—seem beauteously blended together in beautiful symmetry.'

He was undoubtedly a sharp-minded individual, and although he had trained in London as a lawyer (starting his own law practice whilst still in his twenties), God obviously had other plans for him. Converted at John Street Chapel whilst in London, Robert was taken under his pastor's wing and was mentored in preaching. And as the young man's passion for Christ and making Him known increased, so his interest in law and business decreased.

Church leadership

Aged twenty-nine, he received a call to pastor a small Baptist chapel in Barnstaple, Devon, little realizing that he would be entering the lions' den. But neither he nor its members could have imagined that his ministry there would continue for the next seventy years! Ebenezer Baptist Chapel had been a hotbed of conflict and had seen off three pastors in the eighteen months prior to Chapman's call. Things didn't look too hopeful when he arrived and the realization dawned that his theological convictions were significantly different from those held by the church. Another short pastorate threatened. However, through his determined, tender and consistent teaching of the Word week by week, the people took both to the young man and to his doctrine. He taught them in life as well as in speech that 'Love . . . always protects, always trusts, always hopes, always perseveres. Love never fails' (1 Cor. 13:7–8). In days when Christians have come to believe that ego, personality and self-promotion are par for the course in church life, the pattern for leadership Robert Chapman provides is invaluable. Not that he was theologically limp, or lacking strength of conviction—far from it. He didn't budge from his firm biblical convictions but, even when drawn into necessary theological controversy, although often grieved by the harm done because of the obstinacy of some church leaders, he remained characteristically kind, patient and loving, so that even those whom he had to oppose had love and respect for him. He was catholic in the true sense of the word: Chapman loved the church—the whole church of Jesus Christ. He did not love just one party or sect within it, but his heart went out to all who were in Christ's family. 'Whatever name they took, he welcomed them.'[4] He undoubtedly heeded the apostle Paul's words that 'the Lord's servant must not be quarrelsome but must be kind to everyone, able to teach, not resentful. Opponents must be gently instructed, in the hope that God will grant them repentance leading them to a knowledge of the truth' (2 Tim. 2:24–25).

The way of love

'Live a life of love, just as Christ loved us and gave himself up for us as a fragrant offering and sacrifice to God' (Eph. 5:2). Here the apostle Paul charges us to recognize that the Christian life must be 24/7, and the life of Robert Chapman helps us to see what that actually looks like. He practised love to all people and in all situations. He was an overflowingly generous man, giving to the needy often—on one occasion he literally gave the coat off his own back. Although a lifelong bachelor, he was rarely alone, his home always open. One particular guest provides us with a beautiful insight into the man's home—and heart: 'He attends to the minutest bodily and spiritual wants of a stream of visitors, some of whom stay for an hour, some for a month.' All his guests told of his custom of cleaning their shoes. After showing them to their rooms, their host would instruct them to leave their shoes outside their doors. By morning, they would be cleaned.

Love for enemies

It is hard to see how one so loving could ever have had an enemy. But then we just need to remember how so many detested and ill-treated our Saviour. A grocer in Barnstaple came to despise Ebenezer's pastor and was so disturbed by his open-air preaching that on one occasion he spat on him. For some years, the tradesman continued to attack and criticize him, yet the preacher continued to take every opportunity he could to reach out to his detractor, looking for any possible way he could bless him. An opportunity arose when a wealthy relative came to stay with Chapman. Touched by his host's modest home and lifestyle, and clearly moved by his simple trust in God to meet his needs, the relative, as he was leaving, asked if he could buy groceries for Chapman. Chapman agreed, but on the condition that they were purchased at a certain grocer's store—the one owned by the man who so strongly vilified him. The relative, totally oblivious to the tensions that existed between the two men, visited and paid for the food at the store. When instructed to deliver the substantial delivery to 'R. C. Chapman', the stunned grocer replied by saying that he must have come to the wrong shop. But the relative quickly assured him that this was the very store he had been directed to. The grocer arrived at the house with the goods, and at the sight of Chapman he broke down in tears. He asked Chapman for his forgiveness, and on that very day he gave his life to Christ.

Chapman was highly respected by all who knew of him, even by those who had no time for God, and he would often be referred to as the 'man of God' or 'that holy man'.

Old and full of years

Chapman preached his last sermon (lasting one hour and a quarter) just before his ninety-eighth birthday. A few months later Robert Cleaver Chapman was taken to be with his Lord. Out of fear that the focus would be shifted from his Saviour onto him, he destroyed all the letters he had received, doing all he possibly could to deflect the praise he so often received to the One who loved him and gave Himself for him. Nevertheless, despite all his efforts he was known and loved all around the world. In fact, so well known was he in England that a letter sent from overseas simply addressed to 'R. C. Chapman, University of Love, England' found its way to the right person swiftly and with ease.

GEMS

Humility is the secret of fellowship, and pride the secret of division.

Do we meet with unkindness from brethren? Instead of shooting out bitter words at them, let us judge ourselves; and endeavour, in love and wisdom, to overcome evil with good.

Though Christ can be grieved at a thousand things in us that no eye but His can see, yet none is so easily pleased as He by our little endeavours of love.

Keep low, look up, and press forward.[5]

ENCOURAGEMENT: DAWSON TROTMAN ('DAWS'), THE UPLIFTER
(1906–1956)

In Acts, we read of the man who first came trustingly alongside the violent persecutor Saul, the religious zealot who had professed faith in Christ but whose church he had so opposed and harmed. Joseph, for good reason, was nicknamed and thereafter known as Barnabas, 'Son of Encouragement'. The story is told of how Billy Graham was attending a breakfast for a group of influential men. An observer watched as the waiter brought the bill to the party, and noticed that it was the famous evangelist, although the guest, who quickly reached to settle it first. What impressed the onlooker most, however, was not so much the spontaneous act of generosity, but the way Graham treated the waiter. Even though it had apparently been over a year since he had eaten in that restaurant, he knew the waiter by name and asked specific questions about him and the welfare of his family.

Encouragement takes effort, but it has the elevating effect of making a person feel of worth. It is Christlike in its very nature, and it calls for us to be self-effacing and willing to put ourselves out in order to lift another up. While many know of Billy Graham, one great encourager, far fewer have heard of Dawson Trotman who, after a rocky beginning, would later come to be a great help to the world-famous evangelist.

Reckless youth
Dawson was born on 25 March 1906 in Bisbee, Arizona, and

although not from a Christian home, he attended church on occasion throughout his childhood. As a kid, he was a fun-loving, restless, no-half-measures kind of character, but by his youth he was clearly heading for trouble, stealing, drinking and hanging out in pool bars. These were Prohibition days in America, and just two months after his twentieth birthday Trotman was picked up by law enforcement officers and arrested for being under the influence of alcohol.

On their way to the police station, one of the officers looked at him and said, 'Do you like this kind of life?'

The dishevelled youngster replied, 'Sir, I hate it!'

This was just the kind of shake-up he needed, as following graduation from high school he confessed that he 'could not gain mastery over lying and stealing'. The following weekend, he returned to church, making a sincere but vain attempt at self-reformation. However, it was here that he was encouraged by the Sunday school leader to memorize Bible verses. This was to have an impact none could have imagined, as Scripture memorization was to become his lifeblood as well as his lifeline, and, in years to come, would be the means of blessing to untold thousands.

God's powerful Word

Week after week, Dawson's mind stored Bible verses, until one day the Spirit powerfully brought the truth home to the depths of his being as he mulled over John 5:24 and was forced to ask himself if he really did possess the 'everlasting life' it spoke of. There and then, by the roadside, he prayed, asking God to give him that life from above: 'O God, whatever this means, I want to have it.'

From this point, although employed as an attendant at a service station, he was increasingly being stirred to give out to others what he himself was taking in, and he began to earn a reputation as a soul-winner who loved to nurture and encourage young converts in their new walk with Christ. He then began attending the Bible Institute in Los Angeles, where he befriended a young sailor named Les Spencer, who would be on leave for shifts of six weeks at a time. Les brought a shipmate back to 'Daws' and asked him to teach his pal what he himself had been taught. 'You teach him!' was the immediate response to the sailor's request. It was here that Trotman saw an opportunity to create a 'floating seminary' on board the Navy ships. Les would return on board with new converts who Daws would later invite to stay at his home and further disciple. This was the embryo from which The Navigators would later be born.

A deepening prayer life

Dawson Trotman was a man who buzzed with enthusiasm for life, combining a crazy sense of fun with a blood-earnest seriousness for God and for reaching the lost, and many were drawn to him and his cause through his larger-than-life personality. 'Truth mediated through personality' is always God's method, never overriding how we are created, but sanctifying and using the personality of each one, whether introvert or extrovert. Daws and a small group of others formed the Fisherman's Club who would share their faith on the streets, and in this they all benefited from 'iron sharpening iron' in gospel work. But an even greater influence came from his reading quality books, biographies and books on prayer—

especially E. M. Bounds' classic *Power Through Prayer*. One statement from that book particularly impacted him:

Men are God's methods. The church is looking for better methods; God is looking for better men . . . what the church needs to-day is not more machinery or better, not new organizations or more and novel methods, but men whom the Holy Ghost can use—men of prayer, men mighty in prayer. The Holy Ghost does not flow through methods, but through men. He does not come on machinery, but on men. He does not anoint plans, but men—men of prayer.

Although Trotman spent much time in private prayer, he was never a loner in prayer and delighted to meet with others in seeking God for the lost.

Getting organized

Daws was undoubtedly a disciplinarian, and he had the kind of organizational abilities and ideas that sooner or later would get legs and run. His training programme designed to equip and empower Christians began to develop and grow, and in 1935 he gave his organization its present name, The Navigators, with the motto, 'To know Christ and to make Him known'. A number of tools were designed and made widely available to help others in the task of being disciple-makers, motivated by the apostle Paul's words in his second letter to Timothy, 'And the things you have heard me say in the presence of many witnesses entrust to reliable people who will also be qualified to teach others' (2 Tim. 2:2).

A bigger platform

In 1950, he received an invitation from Billy Graham to help with his city-wide crusades. The evangelist was concerned that the many who responded in his meetings were 'falling through the net' when it came to following them up. With typical humility, Daws declined, feeling he lacked the experience. But Graham would have none of it, and persisted until the reluctant encourager obliged and entered what would be a most fruitful partnership. They became close friends, and Billy would always consult Daws when faced with a major decision. At the funeral of The Navigators' founder, it was he who gave the message, and among the numerous qualities of Daws that he mentioned he referred to his passionate desire to help and encourage others: 'I think Daws has personally touched more lives than anybody I have ever known,' said the man who was used of God in the transformation of millions over the decades.

Dying as he lived

It was 18 June 1956, and Daws was among a small group of people waterskiing on Schroon Lake, New York. Tired after the exertion of their day, they settled to relax in the homeward-bound boat, when it suddenly bounced on a wave, shooting Daws and one of the girls in the party out into the lake. The girl couldn't swim. As the boat circled back to pick them up, the fifty-year-old held her up, out of the water, and she was hauled aboard. But as the group then reached down to hoist up Daws, he had sunk out of sight, and he subsequently drowned. The July issue of *Time* magazine carried an article on his life which closed with the poignant statement, 'He lived to save others.' The caption under his photograph summed up his life perfectly: 'Dawson Trotman—always holding someone up.'

Encouragers wanted

Is there not a desperate need in the church today for encouragers? For gracious, selfless men and women with an eye continually looking for opportunities to 'hold someone up' by speaking a kind word, sending a card, paying a visit or making a phone call, and who, like our Saviour, 'know how to sustain with a word him who is weary' (Isa. 50:4 ESV)? But the thrust of Dawson Trotman's life is impossible to miss: the powerful biblical emphasis of help, advice and encouragement in the Lord given to those who were infants in the faith. Every new convert needs a mentor, one who will come alongside and disciple them in the things of God, leading them on to maturity—a Barnabas- and Dawson Trotman-type man or woman willing to humbly support and encourage. I personally will be forever grateful to the one who not only led me to Christ, but who—despite being a young Christian himself—was a 'personal pastor' at my side, pointing me to the right church, discussing Bible passages with me and suggesting the best books to read: simply 'holding me up'.

GEMS

Never do anything someone else can and will do, when there is so much of importance to be done which others cannot or will not do.

How do you know if you are a servant? By how you react when someone treats you as one.

You can lead a soul to Christ in from twenty minutes to a couple of hours. But it takes from twenty weeks to a couple of years to get him on the road to maturity, victorious over the sins and the recurring problems that come along.

The curse of today is that we are too busy. I am not talking about being busy earning money to buy food. I am talking about being busy doing Christian things. We have spiritual activity with little productivity.[6]

DETERMINATION: GLADYS AYLWARD,
THE LITTLE DYNAMO
(1902–1970)

'In 1930, a petite parlor maid told her parents: "Never get me out, or pay ransom for me. God is sufficient." She then set out from London to China with a bedroll, a kettle, a saucepan, a suitcase of canned food, a little change, and much religious fervor.' So began a news report in the *New York Times* at the death of Gladys Aylward on 3 January 1970.

Humble beginnings

Gladys Aylward was born into a working-class family in Edmonton, North London, on 24 February 1902. With little education her options were few, but the spirited youngster found employment at the age of fourteen as a domestic maid. Although raised in a Christian home, by her late teens she had become totally indifferent, even intolerant of anything religious. 'Domestics' in England had a tough time just after the First World War, with long hours worked for little pay, but working as a parlour maid would enable Gladys to fulfil her dream of going on the stage. In the evenings, she attended drama classes that would equip her for her future career, but in the meantime, she would journey into London's buzzing West End and queue for hours to purchase a cheap seat to watch a show at the Drury Lane Theatre. This helped feed her dreams of one day herself being in front of the lights, receiving the applause of the spellbound crowds.

Gripped by a higher passion

For some reason—for which she had no earthly explanation—Gladys found herself one night attending a Christian meeting. It was a disturbing experience for the young woman, as a deep struggle for her soul raged. She agreed to meet with a minister and his wife to talk things through, and although there was an absence of any dramatic experience or feeling, she knew she had arrived at the most important of crossroads in her life. 'There, for the first time,' she wrote, 'I realized that God had a claim on my life, and I accepted Jesus Christ as my Saviour.'

Gladys then joined the Young Life Campaign,[7] and when reading their magazine was deeply impressed by an item on China, and the millions there who had never heard of the One who had loved and saved her. The very thought of this moved her to the depths. 'Someone ought to do something!' was her immediate response. So she approached her Christian friends and challenged them, but not one of them was concerned. Appeals to others were met with the same resounding silence. In fact, for the next fourteen months everyone she met was fervently and bluntly confronted with the same challenge.

Finally, her brother was cornered and informed of the desperate need in China, but he replied, 'Not me!' Then, poking his head round the door as he hurriedly exited the room, he shot back teasingly, 'If you really believe somebody ought to be going, why don't you go yourself!'

There was no escaping the force of those words the moment they were spoken. It was Another who was speaking, calling with a voice that was penetrating and persistent, producing in Gladys Aylward an inescapable conviction as the weeks passed that it was indeed she who should 'do something'.

Unqualified and unfit

Gladys could no longer ignore or escape the heavenly pressure placed upon her soul. She decided to approach a missionary society to share her burden for the multitudes in China who were perishing without a Saviour. They sent her to their college for three months, after which she would be informed of the committee's decision as to whether or not they considered her to be missionary material. When the months had passed, Gladys was devastated to be told that they considered she lacked the necessary qualifications, stating that her lack of education would hinder her from being able to learn the Chinese language. Not only that, but she was twenty-eight years old and considered too old for the task.

This may well have deterred a lesser mortal, but the ice that was showered upon this 'Cockney Sparrow' was unable to quench the fire God had lit within her heart. Although momentarily crushed, she came to the decision that if no missionary organization would send her, she would go on her own, saving up all the money she had earnt from working as a parlour maid with the aim of purchasing a one-way ticket to China.

When she arrived at the ticket office, the booking clerk's eyes almost popped out of his head as the tiny young woman before him enquired about the price of a ticket to China—with no return.

'It would be £47.10. But it's too much of a risk, there's fighting in Manchuria,' he warned.

'I'm the one taking the risk,' was the feisty reply. 'Will you let me save for that ticket?'

There was no deterring Miss Aylward, and so she set about

raising the money, praying and dreaming about the adventure she knew God had for her as she stepped out in humble faith and joyful obedience.

Into the unknown

The great day arrived, and Gladys set off on her journey dressed in a reefer coat, orange dress and a jaunty hat, and carrying her two suitcases. Her mother had sought to prepare her for any possible emergency (as mothers do) in which she might be separated from her luggage, and had made pockets in her corset in which to keep her passport, Bible, pen and traveller's cheques. For a missionary setting out for the field in the early twentieth century, in the days before the world-shrinking benefits of the Internet and email, and when telephone communication was pretty basic and restricted, to leave family, friends and familiarity required no small act of faith and commitment. Gladys movingly describes the scene in her own words: 'I set off from Liverpool Street Station at 9.30 a.m. on Saturday October 15, 1932. As the train drew out and I caught a last glimpse of my loved ones, I felt very small and insignificant. Like Abraham and Moses, I had left all behind me and was moving out into a place unknown with only God to help me.'

First labours

Through a meeting in London, Gladys had been put in contact with a seventy-three-year-old missionary in China named Jeannie Lawson, who was desperate for help in operating an inn for mule drivers. So, in that vast unfamiliar country, Gladys headed to Yangcheng in order to commence her first labours. It was there that she began, in the most inconspicuous way, to help the older woman operate an inn for the often-crude travelling mule drivers, whilst learning the Chinese language from these most unlikely teachers. We cannot be reminded too often that God's ways are not ours, and that He is never short of varying the means and methods by which He works. And He seems to sovereignly delight in doing so. After Jeannie's death, the inn was unable to continue for financial reasons, but God was already preparing the next step for His 'little dynamo'.

Foot inspector

In China, having small feet was considered vital for a young woman in finding a suitable husband, so it had long been the appalling tradition for mothers to bind the feet of their daughters to give them a chance in the beauty stakes. Having feet tightly bound from infancy inevitably produced crushed toes, bones and other problems. However, change was in the air, and the authorities were seeking to abolish this form of abuse. In order to achieve this aim, foot inspectors were employed, and a revered and feared mandarin approached Gladys Aylward for the job. But, not one to be intimidated or pressurized, she set out her demands: 'I will do as you wish, Mandarin, but you understand I have come to China to speak about the God I worship. If I inspect the women's feet, I shall use the opportunity to preach in all the lonely villages.' And so she did.

The great trek

As time passed, respect and esteem for this strange diminutive

English woman grew throughout the region. She mastered the language remarkably, and adapted to the vastly different culture. The local people were impressed by her self-sacrificing spirit as they observed how this courageous single foreign woman had risked her life countless times in order to help those in need, even intervening in a volatile riot in a prison.

But, of all her exploits, Gladys is perhaps best known for her twelve-day trek over the mountains. In 1938, Japanese forces invaded the region, and by 1940 the fighting had escalated. It was at this time that, despite being wounded herself, and without food or provisions, she led over one hundred orphans to safety, caring for them every step of the way.

A large heart beat within that tiny frame, and although she never married, she would adopt many war orphans, all of whom would lovingly regard her as 'Mother'. A good number of them would later testify how they came to Christ through her influence.

Unwanted fame

On returning to England, Gladys was embarrassed to discover that she had become a celebrity, with TV programmes, numerous books and even a Hollywood movie made about her life. The short, dark, plain-looking missionary was especially upset by the liberties taken by 20th Century Fox casting the tall, blonde, attractive Swedish actress Ingrid Bergman to portray her in *The Inn of the Sixth Happiness*, as well as by a number of inaccurate and inappropriate portrayals of her life and work which she felt were detrimental. After ten years, she sought to return to China, but entry was refused by the government, so she settled in Taiwan in 1957, where she founded the Gladys Aylward Orphanage. Although often speaking about her beloved China when opportunities arose, it was there she worked until her death in 1970. Up to the end, she could never quite get over the fact that God would use her. Commenting to a friend she said,

I wasn't God's first choice for what I've done for China. There was somebody else. I don't know who it was—God's first choice. It must have been a man—a wonderful man, a well-educated man. I don't know what happened. Perhaps he died. Perhaps he wasn't willing. And God looked down and saw Gladys Aylward, and He said, she's willing.

And willing she certainly was.

Gems

If God has called you to China, or any other place, and you are sure in your own heart, let nothing deter you . . . remember it is God who has called you, and it is the same as when he called Moses or Samuel.

Here I was worrying about my journey, while God was helping me all the way. It made me realize that I am very weak; my courage is only borrowed from Him, but, oh, the peace that flooded my soul . . . because I know that He never faileth. I would not, if I could, turn back now, because I believe that God is going to reveal Himself in a wonderful way.

[Written in a letter to a struggling teenager:] Don't worry about your education. God won't ask you for certificates; He'll only ask you if you've been faithful to your call.

Oh, God, here's my Bible. Here's my money. Here's me. Use me God.[8]

Courage: Martin Luther, God's disturber (1483–1546)

It is often the case that when the church is in crisis, God raises up the right person, at the right time, in the right place for a specific purpose: 'Cometh the man, cometh the hour.' This was certainly the case in sixteenth-century Germany, when corruption was rife in the church and darkness seemed to reign. Looking back through the centuries, we recognize Martin Luther indisputably as a man of giant intellect and a colossus of courage, but a person is not made in a day. We ourselves may not be earth-shaking reformers, but the God who shaped a Martin Luther is no less meticulous in shaping you and me for our own particular mission here on earth. 'For we are God's handiwork, created in Christ Jesus to do good works, which God prepared in advance for us to do' (Eph. 2:10).

Early days

Born of peasant stock in the small mining town of Eisleben in central Germany on 10 November 1483, Martin Luther soon gave evidence that he was a child of no ordinary intelligence. He was raised by his parents, Hans and Margarete, in the strict, if not reassuring disciplines of the Roman Catholic Church. When Martin was of age, his father, with high aspirations for his son, enrolled him at the University of Erfurt, entertaining hopes that he would eventually attain a lucrative career in law. Applying himself to his studies, Martin received a Bachelor of Arts degree in 1502 and then a

Master's in 1505. Hans, however, was slightly concerned at the boy's rather excessive interest in religion.

Significant storm

It was in 1505 that an incident occurred that was to prove to be the small hinge that would turn a massive door. Whilst walking back to university from visiting his parents, twenty-one-year-old Martin was caught in a severe storm, and a lightning bolt struck so near to him that he was knocked to the ground. Believing that death was imminent and that he was about to enter an uncertain eternity with no priest there to issue the last rites or hear his final confession, he cried out, 'Saint Anne, help me! I shall become a monk!' But when he informed his father of his freshly made vow, he encountered another storm. Hans was livid, feeling that he had wasted all the money spent on his son's education, just to have him throw his life away in some religious order. But keep his promise Martin did, and just two weeks later he entered the Augustinian monastery in Erfurt.

Monastic life

Desperate for inner peace, the new candidate discovered that he had simply entered a world of rules, offering a righteousness that no human being could attain. Looking back later in life, he would write of that period, 'When I was a monk, I wearied myself greatly for almost fifteen years with the daily sacrifice, tortured myself with fastings, vigils, prayers, and other very rigorous works. I earnestly thought to acquire righteousness by my works.' Luther had no idea of the true Christ, seeing Him only as 'a severe and terrible

Judge portrayed as seated on a rainbow'. He was ordained to the priesthood in 1507, but when celebrating his first mass he stood by the altar and, gripped by fear, cried in terror, 'Who am I that I should lift up mine eyes or raise my hands to the divine majesty? For I am dust and ashes and full of sin, and I am speaking to the living, eternal and true God.'

Still no peace

Still pious, the troubled monk continued in his desperate search. Although forbidden the private study of the Bible, he spent his spare hours poring over the Scriptures, and whilst doing so built up an extensive knowledge of them. But then, in 1510, it seems that mercy shone upon him, and he was sent on monastery business to Rome. Surely being there, so near to the saints and apostles, and in a place so packed with relics and riches, his soul could not fail to prosper, he reasoned. On his arrival, he prostrated himself on the ground, then headed off on a whirlwind tour of the holy sites, stocking up on merit at one place after another—or so he hoped. Not wishing to miss out on any possibility of acceptance with God, he decided to climb the Scala Sancta—the staircase which Jesus allegedly climbed in Jerusalem to appear before Pontius Pilate. He ascended on his knees, kissing each step and saying the Lord's Prayer for each one as he climbed. And yet, after all of that, when he reached the top he dejectedly asked himself, 'Who knows whether it is true?'

In 1512, Luther received his Doctor of Theology degree from the University of Wittenberg and became a teacher of the Bible there—remarkably, a position he retained for the next thirty-four years, until his death. But still the one question that consumed his every thought was, 'How could a sinful man ever be made right before a holy God?'

Flashpoint

Although the church continued to parade its collection of relics and wonders—a fragment of bread from the Last Supper, an assortment of oddities such as the teeth and bones of the saints, and a wisp of straw from the crib of Jesus—the final straw was to come in the form of a wily itinerant Dominican friar who sought to make money from indulgences. This scam had been operating for some time to raise money to fund the Crusades. The people were encouraged to purchase a letter from the church that allegedly could free a dead loved one from purgatory. Along came Johann Tetzel, 'the travelling televangelist of indulgences',[9] selling his wares, in this case to pay for a new St Peter's Basilica in Rome. He was undoubtedly a great marketing man and brought his own 'jingle' to help sales: 'As soon as the coin in the coffer rings, the soul from purgatory springs.' This was an absolute outrage to the pious (yet still unenlightened) monk, who was convinced that there must be a public debate on the matter.

The Ninety-Five Theses

On 31 October 1517, Martin Luther nailed his list of Ninety-Five Theses—or statements—regarding indulgences to the front door of the Castle Church in Wittenberg. This was no fuming, 'throwing a wobbly' incident, but simply the 'done thing' when issuing an invitation to debate. But Luther's words were hitting the church where it hurt most—its pocket. As a result, within weeks, the act 'went viral'. Luther became the people's hero, and essentially it was this act that kickstarted the Reformation. The juggernaut started rolling, with the local archbishop complaining to the pope. But this only confirmed the dissenter in his resolve, and he began to attack the infallibility of the pope—an act that was not likely to be tolerated.

His tower experience

Remarkably, as yet, it is most likely that Luther was still not converted. In the midst of the mounting maelstrom, there was a still greater one raging within him: how could he, a sinner, be acceptable to a holy God? He became obsessed with Romans 1:17: 'For in the gospel the righteousness of God is revealed—a righteousness that is by faith from first to last, just as it is written: "The righteous will live by faith."' Up until then, Luther had understood the righteousness of God as that righteous anger against his sin, so therefore he hated the very thought of it, and could only shrink in horror from such a God. However, one day, whilst sitting in the tower of the Castle Church in Wittenberg, meditating on the meaning of this text, the light flashed on. He later wrote,

There I began to understand that the righteousness of God is that by which the righteous person lives by a gift of God, namely by faith. And this is the meaning: the righteousness of God is revealed by the gospel, namely, the passive righteousness with which a merciful God justifies us by faith, as it is written, 'He who through faith is righteous shall live.' Here I felt that I was altogether born again and had entered paradise itself through open gates.

'Here I stand'

In the summer of 1520, the pope issued a papal bull in which he referred to Luther as a wild boar that had invaded God's vineyard, and that forty-one of Luther's teachings were heretical. Luther was given sixty days to repent or face excommunication. He responded by burning the solemn decree—and all Germany waited with bated breath as to the next move against this monk who had dared to challenge the unassailable organization of the Roman Church. The following year, Luther was summoned by the young Holy Roman Emperor, Charles V, to appear before the Diet of Worms in order that he might publicly recant of his heresy. Much was at stake: he was to face the wrath of the emperor, the pope, burning at the stake, and, of course, eternal hell, if proved wrong. Standing alone before such an august assembly, the renegade monk was asked whether he was willing to retract his teachings. The next day, he replied in these now memorable words:

Unless I am convinced by the testimony of the Scriptures or by clear reason (for I do not trust either in the pope or in councils alone, since it is well known that they have often erred and contradicted themselves), I am bound by the Scriptures I have quoted and my conscience is captive to the Word of God. I cannot and I will not recant anything, since it is neither safe nor right to go against conscience. I cannot do otherwise, here I stand, may God help me, Amen.

Luther did indeed stand, and 'Here I stand' would become the battle cry of the Reformation.

The monk marries

In 1525 Luther married Katherine von Bora, an incredible character and a suitable match for Martin. A former nun, she had escaped the monastery and renounced her monastic vows in order to be the Reformer's wife and then mother to their six children. Theirs was a happy home, and Katherine ('Dear Kate', as Luther would call her) was a fine picture of the noble wife of Proverbs 31, taking care of their holdings and the breeding and selling of cattle to provide for the family, as well as providing hospitality for the endless stream of visitors seeking audience with her husband.

Fighting the good fight

For the remainder of his days, Luther continued his work of preaching, writing, lecturing, debating and, of course, battling. Not surprisingly, there was a price to pay for such pressure, and he became subject to a number of illnesses, among them loss of sight in one eye and painful gallstones, which he endured for his final fourteen years.

Martin Luther was a blunt man, to put it mildly. His speech could at times be crude and coarse, and he was far from being the clean-cut Christian hero we perhaps would prefer. But what cannot be doubted is that Luther was God's man for the hour—God's disturber: an ox-like character who was far from perfect, an 'earthen vessel', and yet, in the hands of God, mightily used to fulfil His purposes. Engaging in the battle for truth is never an option. It is always our duty to ensure that the gate to salvation—justification by faith in the merits of Christ alone—is never obscured.

Upon his death, wife Katherine summed up Luther's life well, even though unable to foresee the full impact her husband's work would have: 'Who would not be sad and afflicted at the loss of such a precious man as my dear lord was . . . He did great things not just for a city or a single land, but for the whole world.'[10]

Gems

From the beginning of my Reformation I have asked God to send me neither dreams, nor visions, nor angels, but to give me the right understanding of His Word, the Holy Scriptures; for as long as I have God's Word, I know that I am walking in His way and that I shall not fall into any error or delusion.

Faith is a living, daring confidence in God's grace, so sure and certain that a man could stake his life on it a thousand times.

I have held many things in my hands, and I have lost them all; but whatever I have placed in God's hands, that I still possess.

You are not only responsible for what you say, but also for what you do not say.

KINDNESS: AMY CARMICHAEL,
GENTLE WARRIOR
(1867–1951)

The little girl was excited to be taken by her mother for 'grown-up' tea and biscuits in a Belfast tea shop. As they ate, the girl watched with sadness as a tiny, dirty beggar girl pressed her nose up against the window, looking longingly into the attractive, brightly lit tea shop at all the cakes and sweets on display. Young as she was, little Amy made a promise that when she grew up she would give her money to the poor. Even then, it seems that God was at work, giving Amy Carmichael a caring and compassionate heart—as well as a beautiful poetic gift. Later that day, sitting at home by the fire, she wrote:

When I grow up and money have,
I know what I will do;
I'll build a great big lovely place,
For little girls like you.

But perhaps it is possible to trace God's equipping for her life's work even before that incident. Among Amy's first memories were of when, as a three-year-old, she pushed a chair up to a chest of drawers and peered into the mirror full of expectation, only for her anticipation to turn to disappointment. As she looked at the colour of her eyes, she saw that they were brown. But she had prayed so hard that they would turn to blue. Although she was quick to recover from her disenchantment, only years later would she fully appreciate the wisdom of God, when being eagerly watched by the assembly of children under her care, every one of whom was brown-eyed. Dohnavur village in Tamil Nadu, India, is where Miss Amy Carmichael of County Down, Northern Ireland, began rescuing children in need. In due course she would build up a large Christian community, and she remained at Dohnavur for the rest of her life, dying there in 1951 without ever returning to Ireland.

The shaping of a life

Born in the small village of Millisle to devout Presbyterians David and Catherine Carmichael, Amy was the eldest of their seven children. Her father died when she was eighteen, plunging the family into financial danger. Providentially, support came in the form of a widower, Robert Wilson, who was co-founder of the Keswick Convention. Later, when Amy was in her early twenties, Wilson asked to be allowed to adopt her, for he felt a special fondness for her after the loss of his only daughter. So it was that Amy went to live with Mr Wilson and his sons, to work as his secretary. The job put Amy in direct contact with many of the missionaries around the world, including Hudson Taylor, founder of the China Inland Mission (now OMF). This was no doubt instrumental in pressing upon her the call to missions work.

Eternal vision

Although having served zealously as a young woman, taking the gospel to the 'shawlies'—poor women who worked in the Manchester mills—Amy was an unlikely candidate for the life of a missionary. She suffered from neuralgia, which caused her to have to spend entire weeks in bed. Also, she felt reluctant to leave Robert Wilson (whom she fondly called the D.O.M—'Dear Old Man') as the two of them had grown extremely attached to each other. Yet the call of Christ upon her would not go away. Around this time she wrote to her mother:

Everything, everything seemed to be saying 'Go', through all sounds the cry seemed to rise, 'Come over and help us.' Every bit of pleasure of work which has come to me, has had underlying it the thought of those people who have never, never heard of Jesus. Before my eyes clearer than any lovely view has been the constant picture of those millions who have no chance, and never had one, of hearing of the love which makes our lives so bright.

Frustration

Aged twenty-four, Amy set off for Japan, seen off by a party which included Hudson Taylor and the eminent preacher and evangelist F. B. Meyer. But it would not be until later that she would find her lifelong vocation in India. With God, however, there are no mistakes when a life is offered up to Him for service, wherever that may be, and although she served in Japan for only fifteen months, it would prove to be a time of growth and learning, and it was here that she began wearing traditional dress—an innovative practice she would continue when in India. But severe health issues brought her time in Japan to a close, causing her to return to the UK for medical attention. One year later, after working briefly in China, Amy set sail for India, where she would spend her first years involved in evangelism, which was her passion. But by 1901, her focus had taken an unexpected turn.

Rescue

Although her heart was fully set upon itinerant evangelism, her learning of the plight of children who were taken to live in Hindu temples and sentenced there to a life of wicked abuse was something she could not ignore. She recorded in her diary concerning a nine- or ten-year-old girl she found who had been drugged and was lying dead on the floor, 'Heard that the child had been married [to the god], had lived for a year, then died in such agony that the one who was responsible fled from the house with his hands over his ears to shut out the sound of her screams.' Amy had once been asked if her life work could possibly be with children, to which she had strongly replied, 'No.' But it was then that her mind flitted back to that day in the tea shop in Belfast, and she thought, 'I had entirely forgotten this promise.' But there is One who remembers even a child's promise. And though the little girls who would come to her 'great big lovely place' would not be in the least like the poor little Irish girl, yet they were in need. 'And the wonderful thought of our Father was far, far greater than mine.'

Into battle

When considering the challenge facing Amy Carmichael, it is no surprise that she viewed the missionary as a soldier, and we find the theme of battle woven throughout her writings. The enemy is fierce and comes in a multiplicity of guises. At the beginning, even Christians were against her intervention, thinking that she was exaggerating the situation. But the things that went on behind the scenes were truly awful. From this point forward, her life would be devoted to harnessing a group of dedicated women to join with her in the rescue of these children being used as sex slaves, and bringing them into the love and warmth of a home that would be called the Dohnavur Fellowship.

The Dohnavur Fellowship

Dohnavur is situated in Tamil Nadu, just thirty miles from the southern tip of India. Under Amy's loving guidance, the fellowship would become a place of sanctuary for more than one thousand children who would otherwise have faced the bleakest of futures. In an effort to respect Indian culture, members of the organization wore Indian dress and the children were given Indian names. She herself dressed in Indian clothes, dyed her skin with coffee, and often travelled long distances on India's hot, dusty roads to save just one child from suffering. Their first child, Preena, was seven years old and had escaped from a temple where she was being trained for a life as a cult prostitute; she begged to be protected. It was in Dohnavur that the Indian children were educated and trained and would then serve God as Christian nurses, teachers and evangelists. These children and workers became Amy's family. All the children fondly called her *Amma*, 'mother'. Throughout Amy's life, the love of God within her was like a powerful magnet, and children seemed irresistibly attracted to her—so much so that the Hindus were suspicious and began to call her 'the little child-catching Missie Ammal', convinced that she was using a mysterious drug in order to draw them.

Caste system

Amy was determined to fight against the horrors of the caste system. In the Indian caste system, a person's life is valued according to different levels, depending entirely on the family they were born into. The castes range from a person of very high importance and value (Brahmans, who are political and religious figures), down to the people who, according to the system, don't deserve a caste and are simply the Untouchables/Dalits (usually maintenance workers). Incredibly, a mother would rather see her child die of an incurable disease than allow it to be seen by a doctor of a lower caste. Then, of course, there was the horror of newborn children being sold to work as prostitutes in the temples for their entire lives. Ironically, as Amy fought the caste system of India, she found herself also fighting the caste system that the *missionaries* had created in their own communities, which also began with those of high importance and value (themselves), followed by the Christian Indians (their servants/slaves), then the non-Christian Muslims/Hindus, and, finally, the children of India. Amy knew she needed to break both systems, because God loves all people and sent His Son to die for all, including the Untouchables and the children of India.

A loving shelter

Dohnavur's reputation began to spread. Amy encouraged families to bring their newborn girls, simply because girls were considered to be of no value. Inevitably, after just a few short years, the Carmichael 'family' grew and grew. Property was purchased, then a small village was created to accommodate the growing band. The following story not only provides us with a glimpse into the godly atmosphere of the Dohnavur Fellowship, but also reveals something of the heart of this 'gentle warrior'.

'*Amma*?' queried a small voice.

Amy put down her pen and looked up from her writings: 'Yes?'

A very small, thin girl entered Amy's room, and tiptoed her way onto Amy's lap. The girl was six years old, though she appeared to be only a toddler because of her small frame. 'Tell me again how I became your little girl, *Amma*,' requested the little girl as she put her arms around her *Amma*'s neck in a loving embrace.

Amy sighed, put her biography away, and started: 'Well, my precious Gem, you were only just short of two months old when your real *Amma* died of a jungle fever. Your Papa, although he loved you dearly, was going to give you to a local temple, to make the gods of his religion happy.'

The small girl's eyes opened wide with horror: 'What would I do there, *Amma*?'

Amy continued, wishing her daughter wouldn't have to know such things so early. 'Well, the temple priests would never let you play in the sunshine like you do here, and they would teach you dreadful things. Then you would eventually be "married" to the false gods, and would become a prostitute in "honour" of the gods. But God was watching over you, my dear Gem, He knew you needed to become my daughter. So through your aunt, He brought you to me, and now I am your *Amma*, and you are my precious daughter.'

Satisfied with the story, the little girl bounced off to go and play with another of *Amma*'s one hundred 'daughters'.

ICE AND FIRE

Final years

It was in 1931 that Amy earnestly prayed, 'God, please do with me whatever you want. Do anything that will help me to serve you better.' That same day she fell, suffering fractures that would cripple her for the rest of her life. She spent most of her remaining twenty years bedridden in chronic pain, confined to her room at Dohnavur. Not one to be discouraged or bitter when faced with pain or persecution, she remained sweet in her spirit, and her growing family had continual freedom to enter her bedroom and share their hearts with their beloved *Amma*. She now had the quiet times that allowed her to write the books, poems and letters that would be translated and shared around the world.

Amy Carmichael's missionary career in India lasted over fifty-five years without a furlough. Her writings not only encourage, but also serve to convict us today of our too-casual approach regarding the dark powers we have to combat in spiritual warfare, and her life remains a challenge to us all, regardless of where our 'front line' of service may be.

Amy received a letter one day from a young lady who was considering life as a missionary. She asked Amy, 'What is missionary life like?' Amy wrote back saying, 'Missionary life is simply a chance to die.'

Despite much pain, she remained loving, tender and fervent until the last, and on 19 January 1951, aged eighty-three, she went to be with the Saviour she had loved and lived for. It was her request that no stone be laid on her grave at Dohnavur, but her beloved children placed a simple bird bath over it, with just one word engraved: *Amma*.

GEMS

O for a passionate passion for souls,
O for a pity that yearns!
O for the love that loves unto death,
O for the fire that burns!
O for the pure prayer-power that prevails,
That pours out itself for the lost!
Victorious prayer in the Conqueror's Name,
O for a Pentecost!

You can give without loving, but you cannot love without giving.

If I can enjoy a joke at the expense of another; if I can in any way slight another in conversation, or even in thought, then I know nothing of Calvary love.

Thank God for the battle verses in the Bible. We go into the unknown every day of our lives, and especially every Monday morning, for the week is sure to be a battlefield, outwardly and inwardly in the unseen life of the spirit, which is often by far the sternest battlefield for souls. Either way, the Lord your God goes before you, He shall fight for you.[11]

CONVICTION: WILLIAM TYNDALE,
COURAGEOUS TRANSLATOR
(1494–1536)

Such is the complexity of life that we are always much too caught up in its details and dramas for it to provide us with any kind of true perspective. Added to that, perhaps a legitimate humility prevents us from imagining the possibility that God might well be accomplishing some mighty thing through our seemingly inconsequential struggles. Some have compared God's mysterious providential workings to the back of a tapestry. 'It appears to be nothing more than a jumble of thread—tangled, frayed, occasionally knotted, and seemingly random. Nothing really makes sense.'[12] This is certainly the case when tracing the work of the Reformation in England, which took a very different form from that which took place on the Continent. If our eyes were to remain upon palaces and pontiffs, we would miss what God was doing quietly, and yet with enormous significance.

Birth and education

The impact and contribution made by William Tyndale is impossible to calculate. He has been called 'the apostle of England', even 'the father of modern English'. He was born into a fairly affluent family of yeoman farmers in rural south-west England in the county of Gloucestershire. William was thoughtful and studious by nature, and his parents had the means to send him to be educated at Oxford University, where he learnt grammar, arithmetic, geometry, astronomy, music, rhetoric, logic and philosophy, and, perhaps most significantly, was privileged to study languages under the finest classical scholars in England. In 1512, he earned his Bachelor of Arts degree, and three years later, in 1515, he not only received his Master's but was also ordained into the priesthood in London. His theological course, however, lacked any systematic study of the Scriptures, essential for equipping the servant of God who has the responsibility of teaching others. He was later to complain, 'They have ordained that no man shall look on the Scripture, until he be noselled [nursed] in heathen learning eight or nine years and armed with false principles, with which he is clean shut out of the understanding of the Scripture.'

Stirrings

Despite moves to ban and burn them, Martin Luther's teachings via his books infiltrated the country, causing quite a stir. In Cambridge, a group of scholars would meet at the White Horse Inn to discuss and debate the German Reformer's ideas. The gathering, which included a good number of future Reformation leaders, was known as 'Little Germany'. Meanwhile, Tyndale had moved back to his native Gloucestershire to take a post as private tutor to the children of Sir John and Lady Anne Walsh at Little Sodbury Manor. It was here that his hospitable employer would have high-ranking deans, abbots and bishops to dine, and Tyndale, occupying the lowliest place at the table but armed with his little Greek New Testament, would enliven the conversation as they ate. Things came to a head when one of the visiting scholars was so enraged by Tyndale that he cried out, 'We had better be without God's laws than the pope's.'

But Tyndale, exercised by the Holy Spirit, responded, 'I defy the pope and all his laws.' He then spoke those now-famous words: 'If God spare my life, ere many years, I will cause a boy that driveth the plough shall know more of the Scripture than thou dost.' He had been launched into his life's work, and from that moment on, his mind was set on translating the Bible from the original Hebrew and Greek into English.

The task begins

For over a century, John Wycliffe's followers had produced copies of the New Testament in English, but these were only handwritten and a rather stilted translation of the Latin Vulgate. Not only could they not be mass produced, but they also contained many unhelpful theological problems that were a result of having been translated from the Latin. For example, 'do penance' (the Vulgate of Matt. 3:2 and 4:17) would later be translated 'repent', which would set the reader free to bypass the priest and confession, going directly to God for forgiveness. The way of salvation and how to live the Christian life would look altogether different. It is no wonder, then, that Tyndale and his work were considered 'dangerous'. Perhaps in our day we find it hard to believe that there was a time when a person could be convicted of heresy, then be burnt at the stake in England for reading a Bible in their native language. But such was the influence the Roman Catholic Church still exerted at this time. (On 4 April 1519, a woman and six men were burnt in Coventry for teaching their children the Lord's Prayer, the Ten Commandments and the Apostles' Creed in English.)

In April 1524, the thirty-year-old sailed for the Continent to commence his work of translation and publishing, but never would he see England again. His final twelve years on earth would be lived in exile as a much-wanted outlaw. Tyndale began by translating the New Testament, a translation which was regarded as most accurate and readable. To give an idea of timescale, he completed this work in Cologne in 1525, where, just four years earlier, Luther had made his 'Here I stand' declaration. The German Reformer had by this time been extricated from the pope's authority and control. (It was in this same year that Luther produced his famous work *On the Bondage of the Will*.)

Skullduggery

No work of God ever goes unopposed, and that was certainly true of this crucial work for the kingdom and the bringing of such light into the darkness. The brave-hearted translator found a printer to publish his New Testament, but secrecy was of the essence here. However, news of the project leaked out. A bitter opponent of the Reformation, John Cochlaeus, a priest, overheard the conversation of some printers and plied them with wine, after which the secret spilled out that the translation was in the press and almost completed. Startled by such news, Cochlaeus informed the magistrates, demanding that the sheets be seized, and sent a messenger to the English bishops warning them of the danger. Fortunately, Tyndale was tipped off regarding the raid. He gathered the material that had been printed—only ten pages—then ran out into the night, fleeing to Worms, a city buzzing with enthusiasm about Luther and the Reformation. It was here that the printing of the New Testament in the English language was at last completed. Tyndale then began to set about shipping his explosive materials to England.

Contraband

Aware that the authorities had been alarmed, much 'shrewd as serpents' wisdom was required. So, in boxes, barrels, bales of cloth, sacks of flour and in any other possible secret place that could be thought of, the books were hidden and eventually delivered around the country—in spite of the efforts of the eagle-eyed clergy watching at the ports, hoping to intercept them. Tyndale's New Testaments were widely scattered—the demand was remarkable, and they were available at a price within reach of all. But the Archbishop of Canterbury and the Bishop of London were furious and attempted to destroy all the copies they could find, declaring it a serious crime to buy or sell the translation. In 1526, Bishop Tunstall issued a warning to booksellers and had copies burned in public. But the floodgates had been opened, and nothing could hold back the flow of demand.

Roller coaster

The hunt was on, and on 18 June 1528, Cardinal Wolsey, Archbishop of York, dispatched three agents to the Continent for an aggressive search of the dangerous fugitive. But it was to no avail, as Tyndale had moved on to seek refuge in the German town of Marburg. The search continued, but he remained in Marburg, where he used the time well, teaching himself Hebrew, a language he had not been taught in England as a young student. With this newly acquired skill, Tyndale began translating the Pentateuch, the first five Old Testament books, from Hebrew into English, and his productivity increased. In 1529, the intrepid translator moved from Marburg to Antwerp. This thriving city was also something of a refuge as it offered him good printing, sympathetic company and, importantly, a direct supply route to England. Good progress was made, and here he completed the translation of the Pentateuch. But after considering printing in that city too much of a risk, he boarded a ship to Hamburg. However, on the way they were hit by a severe storm off the coast of Holland, the ship was wrecked, and his translation of the Pentateuch was lost at sea. So, after all his efforts, it was back to square one and he faced the task of motivating himself for the laborious work of translating the Pentateuch from scratch once more. This he did when he eventually arrived in Hamburg, where he was taken into the supportive home of the von Emerson family. Here he laboured from March 1529 to January 1530, when the first five books of Moses were finally completed and then taken to Antwerp for printing. The contraband was then smuggled into England and distributed.

Betrayal and death

Despite the rising tide of fury and opposition, Tyndale's impact increased and God's faithful servant worked on in exile, translating more of the Old Testament and writing unsettling treatises. (One of these, *The Practyse of Prelates*, he wrote opposing Henry VIII's planned annulment of his marriage to Catherine of Aragon in favour of Anne Boleyn, on the grounds that it was unscriptural.) But his enemies were many, and a price would have to be paid for such rebellion:

plans were laid to ensnare the man who was the cause of such upheaval. The main player in the treacherous plot was found. Harry Phillips came from a wealthy and notable family, but had worked himself into a corner through gambling, which produced in him a desperation that made him vulnerable to corruption. An unknown figure in the church offered him a large sum of money to travel to the Continent to find and then befriend William Tyndale. This he managed to do, and after winning Tyndale's trust, he one day lured him into a narrow passage where soldiers were waiting to pounce on him and arrest him. After twelve years on the run, the fugitive was captured. He was tried on a charge of heresy in 1536 and condemned to be burned to death. Despite the efforts of Thomas Cromwell to have him spared, the courageous translator was publicly strangled to death while tied to the stake and then burned. His final, famous words were, 'Lord, open the King of England's eyes!'

Two years later, his dying prayer was answered and a copy of the Scriptures was placed in every parish church in England. How lightly we take the privilege of owning our own copies of the Bible, so easily reading that which faithful souls died to give us.

GEMS

I call on God to record against the day we shall appear before our Lord Jesus, that I never altered one syllable of God's word against my conscience, nor would do this day, if all that is in earth, whether it be honour, pleasure or riches, might be given me.

If God be on our side, what matter maketh it who be against us, be they bishops, cardinals, popes, or whosoever names they will?

Christ is with us to the world's end. Let His little flock be bold therefore.

There is no work better than to please God; to pour water, to wash dishes, to be a cobbler, or an apostle, all are one; to wash dishes and to preach are all one, as touching the deed, to please God.[13]

PRAISE: BILLY BRAY,
THE HAPPY MAN
(1794–1868)

'His eye had a merry twinkle, his countenance an open and benevolent expression, his voice a cheerful and pleasant ring . . . ' Billy Bray was determined that, if all other tongues were silent, his, at least, should sing God's praise. If all other hearts were dull, cold and hard, his should glow and flame with fervour and devotion, for he was an adopted son of God, the King of kings. Therefore, he was a prince, already possessing royal rights and privileges, and he rejoiced to think that his Heavenly Father had reserved for him eternal glory and joy.

Although he was a man with barely any education, Billy's reasoning is difficult to contest. Although often criticized for his exuberant behaviour, he would not be deterred, and after forty years of consistent Christian living and service he could say, 'They said I was a mad-man, but they meant I was a glad man, and, glory be to God! I have been glad ever since.' But Billy was no empty vessel; even C. H. Spurgeon thought highly of the enthusiastic Cornish miner, speaking of his 'deep piety and unfeigned humility'.

'Very near hell'

One cannot ignore the fact that one of the reasons why Billy Bray so rejoiced in his hope of heaven was because, at one time, he was, to use his own words, 'very near hell'. Never could he get over God's kindness to him: 'The Lord was good to me when I was a servant of the devil, or I should have been down in hell now.' However, very few sink deep into the pit of sin suddenly; the way down is normally a gradual descent, and this was true of Billy.

He was born in the Cornish village of Twelveheads as the eldest child born to Ann and William Bray. William, a miner and pious Methodist, died when the children were young, and they were then cared for by their grandfather. After leaving school, Billy moved away from their godly influence and teaching to Devon, to work as a tin miner. As time passed, his lifestyle became increasingly reckless. Drunkenness— the 'gateway' vice that it is—led to fighting, theft and 'viler sins than any that have been mentioned'. In 1821, he married Joanna, a lapsed Methodist, and they eventually had seven children. But family life failed to restrain this man from his downward trajectory. Twice he was nearly killed, once in a mine accident and again as he drunkenly rode a stolen horse. Reflecting upon those days, he would later say that he was 'the wildest, most daring and reckless of all reckless, daring men'. But God was to shake his life.

One day, there was a terrible accident at the tin mine where Billy Bray worked. The roof of the mine ruptured, just missing him. This incident shook the reprobate deeply; he knew that he would have gone straight to hell had he been killed. Now twenty-nine years old, he was given a copy of the book *Visions of Heaven and Hell* by a friend. He was especially convicted by the description of 'two lost souls in hell, cursing each other for being the author of each other's misery'. What pierced his soul was the thought, 'Shall S. Coad [his friend] and I who like each other so much, torment each other in hell!'

ICE AND FIRE

New creation

There was a deep stirring, not only within Billy's soul, but also within that of his long-suffering wife, Joanna, who, although lapsed, began reminiscing, speaking about 'the sweetness of knowing the Lord'. 'Why don't you begin again?' he found himself asking her. Billy later said that he himself wanted to pray there and then, but pride and the devil kept him from it. However, one night, at about 3.00 a.m., he awoke and knelt by his bedside, asking God to save him. He was a changed man, and experienced the wonderful reality of heavenly transformation that the apostle Paul speaks of: 'If anyone is in Christ, the new creation has come: the old has gone, the new is here!' (2 Cor. 5:17). The next payday, he came home from work sober, having skipped his weekly trip to the bar. His wife was greatly surprised by his early return. 'You will never see me drunk again!' he promised her. However, the enemy of our souls is always filled with fury at the loss of a captive, and Billy was bombarded by arrows of doubt in those early days. But he stood on the promises of God's Word and came through with praise on his lips. He touchingly recalls,

I said to the Lord, 'Thou hast said, "They that ask shall receive, they that seek shall find, and to them that knock, the door shall be opened," and I have faith to believe it.' In an instant the Lord made me so happy that I cannot express what I felt. I shouted for joy. I praised God with my whole heart for what he had done for a sinner like me.

Billy was unable to remember the exact day, but he said, 'I remember this, that everything looked new to me: the people, the fields, the cattle, the trees. I was like a man in a new world.'

Inexpressible and glorious joy

'Though you have not seen him, you love him; and even though you do not see him now, you believe in him and are filled with an inexpressible and glorious joy' (1 Peter 1:8). These words of the apostle Peter could well have been written for Billy Bray. But this was to be no fleeting excitement: to the very end of his life Billy would sing out loud, dance and shout praise to the Lord as he walked through life. Some Christians felt his behaviour inappropriate, but his expressions of joy were never contrived or unnatural; they simply came from the heart of a redeemed sinner genuinely thankful for so great a salvation. 'I can't help praising God,' he argued. 'As I go along the street I lift up one foot, and it seems to say, "Glory!" and I lift up the other, and it seems to say, "Amen!" And so they keep on like that all the time I am walking.' A friend said of him,

Billy was so completely absorbed with a desire to do good—so fired with a zeal for the honour of his Divine Master, so full of pity towards his fellow men, so impressed with a continual sense of God's favour and presence—that without regard to position, rank, character or circumstances, he was ever ready to testify to the reality and blessedness of religion, or to administer such reproof, counsel or warning, as he deemed necessary.

His labours

Billy took Cornwall by storm. He entered into a new life, and what a life it was! He was possessed by a new power, a new Master, and had been given a new motivation. He preached, he prayed, he raised money to build new chapels, he took orphans into his home, he visited the sick, and in all these things, at all times, he exuded the joy of the Lord. He made his spiritual home with a group of Methodists known as the Bible Christians and was a popular preacher on the Methodist circuit. Whenever it was announced that he was coming to preach, the chapel would be crammed full. Billy not only raised the funds to build chapels but he also laboured in the building of them himself. In fact, a number of 'Billy Bray's chapels' are still standing in Cornwall today. His first—financed through receiving a property from his mother—he cleared with his bare hands, proceeding to then dig out the chapel foundations of what would be called Bethel, 'House of God'.

Child-like faith

There is a humorous incident that demonstrates the Cornishman's cheerful, practical, child-like faith. A chapel he had just built was complete apart for one thing: a pulpit. But time passed and there was still no provision of one. Billy was deeply exercised about this, but one day, whilst walking past some auction rooms, his eyes lit up when he saw a large three-cornered cupboard. 'If I could just lay my hands on that,' he thought to himself, 'I could cut a space in the side, hang a door over the space, put a Bible board on the top, and I would have my pulpit.' On enquiring its price from the auctioneer, he felt sure he would have just enough cash to secure it for his chapel. 'Mercy me,' he thought to himself, 'the Lord has given it into my hand.'

Next day was auction day, and Billy hurried along to the

sale. Soon came the turn for the cupboard to go under the hammer. However, his heart sank as the bidding rose higher and higher, and eventually far above his modest budget. Feeling sure that the Lord was in this, he became perplexed as his 'pulpit' seemed so far from his reach and the cupboard was eventually sold to another bidder.

As he left the auction room, Billy, feeling rather shell-shocked, dreamily happened to follow the purchaser of the cupboard out of the auction rooms to where the item was carefully loaded onto a small barrow and trundled up a hill to its new owner's home. Billy followed on. But upon reaching home, the new owner discovered he had a problem: he was unable to get his new acquisition through the door. Billy heard the man bad-temperedly announce to his wife that he was going to 'chop the thing up for firewood'.

'Please, sir,' said the observer, stepping forward from his viewpoint, 'if it would be more profitable for you to sell the cupboard again, I'll gladly offer you what I've got in my pocket for it.'

'It's a bargain!' said the man. 'And on top of that, I'll take it on my barrow to wherever you want to have it.'

Billy danced with joy as the barrow was trundled back down the hill again towards the chapel—with him still dancing by its side. 'Mercy me, Lord,' he sang, 'Mercy me; Ye knowed that I could never have carried that old cupboard from the auction rooms to the chapel by myself, and so Ye arranged to have it delivered for me. Mercy me!'

It must be remembered that, alongside all his numerous activities, Billy continued working as a miner. But even in the workplace he was as a burning and shining light, claiming he could 'leap and dance for joy underground as well as on the surface'.

'The parson is converted!'

When the new Church of England minister arrived, Billy went to hear 'the parson'. He left the church genuinely saddened, feeling sure that he wasn't a saved man. So, being Billy, he told him so. The following Sunday was remarkable, and best described by Rev. W. Haslam himself, who was famously converted by his own sermon:

> I do not remember all I said, but I felt a wonderful light and joy coming into my soul, and I was beginning to see what the Pharisees [whom he was speaking about] did not. Whether it was something in my words, or my manner, or my look, I know not; but all of a sudden a local preacher who happened to be in the congregation, stood up, and putting up his arms, shouted out in Cornish manner, 'The parson is converted! The parson is converted! Hallelujah!' and in another moment his voice was lost in the shouts and praises of three or four hundred of the congregation . . .

Taken to a higher glory

Print falls painfully short of the mark when seeking to describe such a colourful character, and words are unable to convey the glory that filled his soul. Like us all, he was but a man whose 'flesh and heart must fail'. However, even as his time on earth drew to a close, he continued a passionate, humorous lover of souls. The doctor was sent for, and after he had examined him, Billy enquired, 'Well, doctor, how is it?'

'You're going to die,' the doctor replied solemnly.

Billy instantly shouted, 'Glory! Glory to God! I shall soon be in heaven!' And then he added in a low tone to the doctor, whose spiritual state was in quite some doubt, 'When I get there, shall I give them your compliments, doctor, and tell them you will be coming too?'

The doctor later remarked that the comment made a deep impression upon him. But then, Billy Bray made a deep impression upon many in his day. And in fact, his life of joyful service still resounds today.

GEMS

If they were to put me into a barrel, I would shout out 'Glory!' through the bunghole!

You praise God, and I will praise God, and we will both praise God together.

He has made me glad and no one can make me sad. He makes me shout and no one can make me doubt.

If they were to cut off my feet, I would heave up the stumps![14]

JOY: JONI EARECKSON TADA,
FIGHTER FOR JOY
(1949–)

Once again, I desperately wanted to kill myself. Here I was, trapped in this canvas cocoon. I couldn't move anything but my head. Physically, I was little more than a corpse. I had no hope of ever walking again. I could never lead a normal life and marry Dick . . . I had absolutely no idea of how I could find purpose or meaning in just existing day after day . . . I was despondent, but I was also angry because of my helplessness. How I wished for strength and control enough in my fingers to do something, anything, to end my life.

These are the words of one who later would write, paint, sing and travel extensively for over half a century, touching the lives of millions with her message of hope and demonstrating how it is possible to overcome life's severest trials, through the grace of Jesus Christ. Joni Eareckson Tada is a living sermon, whose life powerfully teaches us that Christian joy is something that comes down from heaven, and is totally independent of earthly circumstances.

That day
It was 30 July 1967, a hot summer's day in Maryland, USA, and seventeen-year-old Joni was full of high spirits. She had just graduated from high school and was packing for college, when sister Kathy invited her to go for a swim at a beach on the Chesapeake Bay. Standing on a short raft anchored offshore, she prepared to dive, never imagining that in the

next second, her life would change for ever. The water was murky and she had failed to realize just how shallow it was. As she entered the sea, her head hit something hard and she immediately felt a sensation like an electric shock, leaving her dazed underwater. Thankfully, Kathy raced to her rescue and pulled her limp body from the dark waters of the bay. The teenager was then rushed to hospital. Confined to a hospital bed and a canvas and metal frame, Joni learned the heartbreaking truth that she would never walk again, nor even have the use of her arms. She had severed her spinal cord, and from that day would be left a quadriplegic, paralysed from the shoulders down and sentenced to a wheelchair for the rest of her life.

The active child

The Eareckson home was a happy one; John and Lindy loved each other and their four daughters. Joni had lived an active, and in many ways idyllic, life, enjoying tennis, swimming and especially her passion: horses. She was an able rider, even at four years old, and gained the distinction of becoming the youngest-ever participant in the one hundred mile 'Cheyenne Ride'. Her father was a gifted painter, and Joni showed the same talent. On a family hike she would take her sketch pad, and, with her father's hand over hers, together they would create some beautiful originals. It was whilst attending a Young Life[15] weekend that she trusted Christ as her Saviour, but she would later write that after her devastating diving accident her 'faith was shipwrecked'. Whilst lying in her hospital bed, she mused, 'If this is the way God treats new

Christians, how could He ever be trusted with another prayer again?'

Watershed prayer

We might well ask, how could a young girl, whose life seemed to have come to an abrupt end, possibly understand why God would allow this to happen? However, Joni had the spiritual awareness to realize that God's ways were far higher than hers, and, quite frankly, where else could she turn? To whom else could she go? But it was here, at her lowest point, that she offered her watershed prayer, 'God, if I can't die, then show me how to live.' As time went by, she would sit in front of a Bible, holding a mouth-stick between her teeth to flip the pages, praying that God would help her put together the puzzle pieces of her suffering, so that she might come to a place of acceptance, if not understanding. 'In acceptance lieth peace,' wrote fellow sufferer Amy Carmichael. After two years of rehabilitation, Joni dug deep into previously untapped reservoirs of grit and determination and, slowly, new skills and abilities began to emerge.

Artist

One of the challenges for her would be how to use her God-given artistic talent. How could a paralysed person possibly ever draw and paint again? But her therapist encouraged Joni to keep painting by learning how to hold the paintbrushes between her teeth. Perspective gained a whole new meaning. She found the hardest part was learning to relax. If her neck or jaw muscles became tense it would be evident in her brush strokes. It was a painstaking process which took Joni several years before she could once again actually enjoy painting. Even for an able-bodied person, hard work and discipline, practice and patience are required, but undoubtedly, her artistic talent did not come from her hands but was a remarkable gift from God. Although at the time it would have been beyond her wildest dreams, she would, in years to come, be a renowned artist whose work would be exhibited all around the world.

Marriage—for better and for worse

Joni had resigned herself to a life of singleness, but God had other plans. In a church service one Sunday she felt distracted, and found herself praying for the dark-haired young man sitting in front. Two weeks later they met at a party. Two years later, Ken Tada and Joni were married.

Their marriage began strong, and, indeed, it needed a special love that would be robust enough to push through the romantic view of 'love' so often portrayed, as Ken would need to take care of all Joni's physical needs. Despite their deep love for one another, there were inevitably demanding challenges for this couple because of Joni's quadriplegia. With the passing of time, Ken found himself overwhelmed by the constant responsibility of caring for a disabled spouse, whilst seeking to work as a high school history teacher. Things climaxed in recent years when Joni was diagnosed with breast cancer, and the chronic pain she experienced exacerbated the tensions already within their marriage, resulting in Ken's sinking into the deep depression he had battled in earlier years. However, they were humble enough to seek outside help and counsel, and are now able to speak openly, not only of the struggles, but also of the victories in their marriage. As a result, the couple have grown closer. 'We strive to be open and honest with each other and solve problems by discussing them, rather than hiding and burying them,' says Joni. 'We pray and read the Bible together and I let my husband keep his dreams.'

Healing?

On occasions—more than she would wish to recall—Joni has been told she lacked faith (even cruelly rebuked) and that if only she had enough faith she would be out of her wheelchair. She recalls how one day, in the early days of her disability, she saw from a TV advertisement that a famous healing evangelist was visiting Washington D.C., so, filled with faith, hope and expectancy, she asked to be taken. As Joni sat in the auditorium that night, the atmosphere was electric. As the evangelist

breezed onto the stage . ... my heart raced as I prayed. 'Lord, the Bible says You heal all our diseases. I'm ready for You to get me out of this wheelchair. Please would You?' But the spotlight always seemed to be directed towards some other part of the ballroom where apparent healings were happening. Never did they aim the light at the wheelchair section where all the 'hard cases' were: quadriplegics like me; stroke survivors, children with muscular dystrophy, and men and women sitting stiff and rigid from multiple sclerosis. God answered. And again, His answer was no. After the crusade I was number fifteen in a line of thirty wheelchair users waiting to exit at the stadium elevator, all of us trying to make a fast escape ahead of the people on crutches. I remember glancing around at all the disappointed and quietly confused people and thinking 'Something's wrong with this picture. Is this the only way to deal with suffering? Trying desperately to remove it? Get rid of? Heal it?'

It's not that Joni believes God cannot or does not heal today; she says, 'God may well miraculously heal, and if He does, it's not only to the benefit of that person but it's to God's glory . . . but, just as in the days of Jesus' earthly ministry, people's physical problems were not His main focus.' She then points to God's great priority: 'The gospel of Jesus says, "Sin kills! Hell is real, but God is merciful! His kingdom can change you, and I am your passport." And whenever people missed this, whenever they started coming to Jesus just to have their problems removed, the Saviour backed away.'

It is no ivory-tower theologian, unacquainted with suffering, who says, 'God does not remove the hardships. He allows them, purposes them, permits, ordains them. Use whichever word you wish. He designs them.' As one who has travelled the path of suffering for over half a century and who has seen the blessing that can result from not being physically healed, Joni's words carry weight.

Joy and blessing

No one could possibly have predicted the worldwide blessing that would result from such a tragic accident that summer's day at Chesapeake Bay. Joni Eareckson Tada has authored over forty books (her first book, *Joni*, has sold more than four million copies and been translated into fifty languages), and she is an internationally known artist, a radio host of a show that reaches over one million listeners a week, and has recorded several music albums. She is founder of Joni and

Friends, a Christian ministry that serves families affected by disability.

July 2017 was the fiftieth anniversary of her life-changing accident. As she reflected upon those fifty years she was remarkably positive: 'Honestly, I'm amazed that the last fifty years feel like only a little while. As I look back, I just see God at work. That's pretty exciting.' However, Joni is a realist and admits that, although with the passing of time she has become used to dealing with the quadriplegia, the pain gets no easier, as it relentlessly invades her life day after day. Each morning at seven, Joni's wake-up crew, affectionately known as her 'Get-up Girls', get her ready—regardless of whether she has slept well or not, whether she's in agony or not, or whether she wants to get up or not. She speaks of her 'hard-fought-for smile, hard-won, and sent straight from heaven . . . I've got joy that's defiant. I've also got joy that's a choice. I decide on it virtually every time I am faced with a day of chronic pain, because pain is the big joy-thief. Pain does everything it can to rob you of your joy in the Lord.'

More than conquerors

Whatever our personal circumstances as we navigate through the inescapable trials and traumas of this troubled world, we have the choice to be either victims or victors. There are many whose lives are scarred because of atrocious acts of abuse, others have endured the trauma of having to flee violence or persecution, and then there is that vast army who daily have to battle with mental health issues. Joni demonstrates that we need not be joyless victims, as God aids us in our conflict as we feed daily upon His Word and are strengthened by the gracious provision of the indwelling Holy Spirit. Joni illustrates this beautifully through an incident that occurred whilst attending a conference in Lausanne:

On the last night our Issue Group, many of whom were disabled themselves, began to pray for healing for those who were ill or in pain. The Holy Spirit then led us to pray for all the nations and people groups that were represented in the room. The power of God's love and joy spilled over. After interceding the group suddenly began to dance whether in wheelchairs, on crutches or on legs in a holy chain of rejoicing in God's overwhelming love. The chain wove through the lobby and able-bodied participants of the Forum joined in or cheered as God was glorified in the praises of His earthen vessels.

This surely is the victory Paul had in mind when he wrote, 'No, in all these things we are more than conquerors through him who loved us' (Rom. 8:37).

Gems

He has chosen not to heal me, but to hold me. The more intense the pain, the closer His embrace.

You want a warrior Jesus . . . You want a battlefield Jesus. You want His rigorous and robust gospel to command your sensibilities to stand at attention.

Heartache forces us to embrace God out of desperate, urgent need. God is never closer than when your heart is aching.

Suffering provides the gym equipment on which my faith can be exercised.[16]

GRIT: WILLIAM BOOTH, GOD'S GENERAL (1829–1912)

While women weep as they do now, I'll fight; while little children go hungry as they do now, I'll fight; while men go to prison in and out, in and out, I'll fight; while there is a poor lost girl upon the street, I'll fight; while there remains one dark soul without the light of God, I'll fight—I'll fight to the very end!

One might be forgiven for thinking these words flowed from the burning heart of a young zealot entering freshly into the work of the gospel, endued with the first flames of zeal and holy ambition. But no. Although coming unquestionably from a heart on fire, this is the red-hot determination of a frail, sick, near-blind eighty-year-old. It was this passion that launched a movement that would have a global impact that is still felt powerfully to this very day, as the Salvation Army carries spiritual and physical hope to millions around the world, even to the remotest places of every continent. But every army needs a general, and William Booth was God's general, raised up to call others to join him in the fierce battle for the souls of men and women.

Eyes opened

William was the second of four children born to Samuel and Mary Booth on 10 April 1829 in Nottingham, a city then of around fifty thousand people. Although Samuel Booth had been a relatively wealthy man by standards of that time, he lost it all and the family descended into poverty. Writing later about his father, William would say, 'My father determined to grow rich, and he did, he grew very rich, because he lived without God and simply worked for money. When he lost it all, his heart broke with it and he died miserably.'

No longer able to afford the school fees, or hope to guide his son into a lucrative business, Samuel Booth sent his thirteen-year-old to be apprentice to a pawnbroker in the poorest district of Nottingham. Although he disliked his job, it was here that William was to have his eyes opened to the plight of the poor and his social conscience stirred. As in other towns and cities at that time, poverty was rife, men were pressed into a life of crime and women into prostitution, whilst murder and arson were frequent events and drunkenness abounded. All this embedded itself into the mind of young William and he would write of 'the degradation and helpless misery of the poor stockingers [weavers] of my native town, wandering gaunt and hunger-stricken through the streets'. He testified to how witnessing these scenes kindled something within, producing deep yearnings that would have a powerful influence upon his future life's direction.

Conversion and calling

William was moved by reading the life of the eighteenth-century evangelist John Wesley. He found his heart drawn out to this man who had a passion for the 'outsiders', those beyond the pale of the 'respectable' Christianity of his day—the majority of whom were illiterate—and who sacrificed reputation and convention in order to reach them. And then he was attracted to John's brother Charles, who wrote hymns that stirred the depths of men and women's emotions and drew them to the Methodist meetings. Ideas as well as passions which would eventually take shape were churning within the young man.

But although he had good desires and motives, there was first a spiritual change needed within the man himself. William had been attending Broad Street Wesleyan Chapel and, although it is difficult to pinpoint his conversion, there are markers. During his fifteenth year he wrote in his diary, 'God shall have all there is of William Booth'; and a short while later, after attending a service one evening, he said, 'It was in the open street that this great change passed over me.' Shortly after this, James Caughey, an American evangelist, visited Nottingham, and Booth was greatly impacted by his powerful preaching; it was at this time that his soul was ignited and a passion to win souls was kindled. Although a shy and self-conscious young man, he felt compelled to go to the city's street corners and preach. Joined by his friend Will Sansom, the pair would take a chair on which to stand and plead with men and women to turn to Christ. Although their early efforts were met with jeers and sometimes bricks from the inhabitants of Nottingham, nothing could douse his enthusiasm; all was simply a foretaste of the battles that would later be fought. William preached his first sermon aged seventeen and was licensed as a Methodist lay preacher by the New Wesleyan Connexion.

All change!

Change was in the air. When William was nineteen, his apprenticeship had come to an end, and as no opportunities were opening for him in Nottingham, after something of a struggle he made the difficult decision to move to London, working reluctantly as a pawnbroker whilst continuing his lay preaching. However, he wasn't content with preaching in churches on Sundays; the sight of London's streets at night, thronging with lost men and women, was too much for him, so he ventured out into the open air, where his increasingly burdened heart was leading him, to take the gospel to those whose last thought would be to enter a church building. At this time, Edward Rabbits, a wealthy businessman and influential member of the Reformers—a group within Methodism seeking to bring the denomination back to its original convictions— was impressed by the earnest young preacher. After observing him for a while, he advised William that he should devote himself fully to Christian ministry as an evangelist, and that he would be willing to support him financially.

It was whilst at a party organized by Rabbits that Booth met the love of his life, and it really was a case of 'love at first sight'. The eye of the tall, hollow-cheeked Booth was caught by a dark, petite young woman by the name of Catherine Mumford, who had already been captivated by the earnestness of the young preacher who had recently visited her church. 'On that day,' he would recall, 'I fell head over heels in love with the precious woman who afterwards became my wife.' They were very soon engaged, and then were married four years later on 16 June 1855. In 'Darkest England' a remarkable partnership was forged that would impact not only the nation, but the whole world for Christ.

Early ministry days

The pair were parted for a period because, with Catherine's

blessing, William accepted a call to pastor a Methodist church in Spalding, Lincolnshire. It was here that he began to hone his evangelistic gift and methods, and he saw God's hand at work quite powerfully, with many coming forward—at times, weeping their way—to the communion rail to commit their lives to Christ. During this period of absence, a number of letters were exchanged between the separated couple, and although they were far from being 'love letters', the relationship was cemented as the months passed. But William began to feel frustrated in the work. Not only was he disillusioned by the politics and various disputes within the denomination, but he also felt a deep yearning for the multitudes outside the churches who remained untouched by the gospel. After eighteen months at Spalding, the young minister resigned, concluding that the 'settled ministry' was not for him.

Returning to London, he embarked upon a course of study at a seminary in Camberwell. But being a 'man of action', he would soon be on the move again, seeking to know where his life's work that God had so laid upon his soul would be. Words spoken at this time provide us with a glimpse into his mind: 'I saw dying souls before me, the gates of Heaven wide open on the one hand, and the gates of Hell open on the other, while I saw Jesus Christ with His arms open between the two, crying out to all to come and be saved.'

'Darling, I've found my destiny!'

Catherine Booth was unquestionably a strong, even dominating character, and William had certainly met his match. But whatever flaws they both had, time would reveal just how God would take hold of this powerful pair to raise an army of fervent followers. Catherine had become a fiery preacher—not without a certain amount of controversy and opposition—but the pair were on a rescue mission, and no one could stop them. William and Catherine became itinerant evangelists in Wales, Cornwall and then the North of England, often preaching in paraffin-lit tents, haylofts, rented rooms, in fact, anywhere they could reach 'outsiders' in order to fulfil Booth's driving ambition to 'Go for souls and go for the worst!' They saw fruit for their labours wherever they went, but the persistent siren voice of London was calling them.

In 1865, the Booths were in their mid-thirties and renting a house in West London. Although engaged in itinerant preaching and missions, William still had not found his niche. One sultry July evening, he wandered through the East End almost in a daze as he took in the raw sights that had caused his soul to be so deeply stirred. The warm night air was thick with the heady stench of smoke, onions, gin and dung, and his heart was heavy as he observed specimens of depraved humanity set before his eyes in every direction. With heart aflame and heedless of the mockery and opposition, the Reverend William Booth lifted up his voice in the open air and offered to them this world's only Saviour.

Meanwhile, at home, with the hours ticking by, Catherine lay wide awake in bed, concerned about her husband, whilst their four children slept, blissfully unaware. With her husband having resigned from the Methodist ministry, their future was increasingly precarious. It was almost midnight, but the man she so deeply loved was missing.

Suddenly, the door opened and in he walked, animated, with eyes aglow. 'Darling,' he said breathlessly, 'I've found my destiny!' Catherine, so wanting to share in her husband's enthusiasm, could feel only the cold touch of uncertainty upon her mother heart.

'Terrible as an army with banners'

Soon after that most significant night, William formed his own East London Christian Mission, which by 1870 was looking rather Methodist-shaped in its structure. Although enjoying a measure of success and expanding, its founder, however, was still not at peace. The mission was failing to attract the 'heathen masses' he longed to reach. Something had to be done. But what?

It was on a May morning in 1878 that the Salvation Army was born—and that quite by accident. There had already been a growing use of military language in the work, but it came to a head that spring day when Booth was dictating a letter to his secretary, George Scott Railton. 'We are a volunteer army,' he said. His son Bramwell, who was listening, jokingly objected, 'Volunteer? I'm no volunteer, I'm a regular!' The Army had been born, and when its leader visited Whitby, a poster was printed announcing Booth as 'The General'. He justified the name in a sentence: 'We are a salvation people— this is our specialty: getting saved and keeping saved, and then getting somebody else saved.'

The transition from Christian Mission to Salvation Army was a smooth one, evidenced by the rapid reorganization as well as by the phenomenal heavenly blessing upon the work. Records show that by the first weeks of January 1879, the General was in command of eighty-two stations, manned by 127 evangelists (100 of them converted at meetings), with

ICE AND FIRE

1,900 voluntary speakers holding 75,000 services a year. In 1880, the Army expanded to the USA, France in 1881, and workers were sent to India in 1882.

War talk

Military language was suitably adopted: a *soldier* served in a local *corps*, working out from its building, a *citadel*, and did *knee drill* when praying. And, of course, after fighting the good fight, a soldier would be *promoted to glory*. An evangelistic newspaper was produced, called *The War Cry*. The Army, now dressed in its distinctive uniform, marched impressively with the startling blood and fire symbolism on its banners: the *blood* of Jesus Christ shed on the cross which alone can bring forgiveness to a sinner, and the *fire* of the Holy Spirit, who alone can create inner purity as He dwells within, enabling us to live lives that are pleasing to God.

But still Booth thought there was a certain magnetism missing that he could not define. And then he hit on that missing piece: the brass band. The first band was formed in Salisbury in 1880 and would be used to stir the passions as the soldiers marched. The General issued guidelines to bandsmen and the songsters (later added) that the songs would be 'simple, strong and soul-saving'. He thought the tunes that accompanied the words were also of importance: 'I rather enjoy robbing the devil of his choicest tunes,' he explained.

Soup, soap and salvation

The compassion Booth had had etched upon his heart for the poor as a young man had not diminished. With his deep conviction concerning the eternal destiny of men and women, he knew only too well that you cannot preach the gospel to a starving man without first giving him food. So from the beginning, only too well aware that they were going to those who often were in dire physical need, the Salvation Army sought to provide for those glaring practical needs, whilst being careful not to neglect the all-important salvation of their eternal souls. Food depots, shelters for vulnerable women, employment bureaux, the Prison-Gate Brigade, 'Slum Sisters', agencies to halt sex-trafficking, and many other supports were put in place in order to combat the poverty and vice that stripped men and women of their God-given dignity. In his typically practical way, to fix the Army's aims firmly in people's minds the General summed up their approach as 'Soup, Soap and Salvation'. It would be God's love in action, a revelation of the One who created man's body as well as his soul.

Fiercely opposed

It is virtually impossible in our day to imagine how this organization, now so loved, could have been so hated and opposed when it began. Ada Smith (whom Booth, no doubt, had in mind when he said, 'Some of my best men are women') enables us to grasp why this was: 'So, with loaded guns and ammunition, we are in the field, and with all our might are pouring red-hot bullets of Calvary, death, judgment, heaven and hell into the ears and hearts of the vast crowds of people, and by the power of God it is taking mighty effect.' Wherever they went they were met with strong opposition. Booth's people faced riots, ridicule, imprisonment, and for some, even death. The soldiers were pelted with rotten vegetables, dead animals, rocks, burning coals and endless verbal abuse. They were opposed by shop keepers, publicans, thugs, and even an organized army called the Skeleton Army, funded by an unlikely alliance of brewers, pimps, businessmen and civil leaders. Such forthright gospel passion not only evoked anger among 'sinners' but also raised the hackles of church leaders, perhaps the most painful of all the attacks the Salvation Army had to endure. 'The Salvation Army stinketh in my nostrils,' said one clergyman, speaking for the many church leaders of the day who opposed them.

Booth's legacy

'What, then, shall we say in response to these things? If God is for us, who can be against us?' (Rom. 8:31). This is always our great bottom line. And there was no power able to withstand God's general and his troops, no matter how they were vilified. By the end of the 1880s, the Salvation Army was an established worldwide organization.

On 20 August 1912, HQ announced that 'The General had laid down his sword'. At eighty-three years of age, having fought a noble battle, the commander was promoted to glory. His body lay in state for three days, after which a crowd of thirty-six thousand packed into a memorial service for him at London's Olympia Exhibition Hall, where twenty-two years earlier a similar throng had attended the funeral of the Army's 'Mother', Catherine Booth.

Though a man of vision, surely Booth could never have imagined the global impact his labours would have. The Salvation Army today works in over 100 countries, with 14,000 Corps. It supervises thousands of food centres, and its hospitals care for twenty-seven million patients annually. Then consider its works among the world's refugees, addicts, prostitutes, homeless and countless other agencies.

Just one person with a passion

All this is a reminder of what God can do through one person with grit and determination, gripped by the love of Jesus, and given wholly to Him for His use. The twenty-first-century church seems strong in emulating William Booth's innovative missional thinking, but do we not today desperately lack his passion for holiness and purity, often placing the pursuit of happiness above holiness? Holiness is the root, and happiness the fruit: it must be that way round, and the Salvation Army exuded joy wherever they went. Booth's own words reveal just where he placed his emphasis: 'The greatness of a man's power is the measure of his surrender.' The founder of this vast Army needed no convincing of the truth of Christ's words, 'Apart from me you can do nothing' (John 15:5), and his dependence upon the Holy Spirit for purity and power is evident in their hymns, especially Booth's pleading, 'Send the fire'. In our necessary caution to avoid a 'two-stage' version of Christianity, could our danger be that we settle for something less than that Holy Spirit-dependent type of faith of past years that has enabled followers of Christ to blaze even in the darkest of hours and situations? It would not be difficult to pinpoint the defects doctrinally, practically and personally in this man and his movement. But our aim here is to confront ourselves with our own failings and defects, and seek to catch something of his flame in order to impact our relatively untouched generation with the gospel. We can do no better than pray the words from Booth's hymn 'Thou Christ of Burning, Cleansing Flame':

'Tis fire we want, for fire we plead,
Send the fire, send the fire, send the fire!
The fire will meet our every need,
Send the fire, send the fire, send the fire!
For strength to ever do the right,
For grace to conquer in the fight,
For pow'r to walk the world in white,
Send the fire, send the fire, send the fire!

GEMS

There are different kinds of fire; there is false fire. No one knows this better than we do, but we are not such fools as to refuse good bank notes because there are false ones in circulation; and although we see here and there manifestations of what appears to us to be nothing more than mere earthly fire, we none the less prize and value, and seek for the genuine fire which comes from the altar of the Lord.

The chief danger that confronts the coming [20th] century will be religion without the Holy Ghost, Christianity without Christ, forgiveness without repentance, salvation without regeneration, politics without God, heaven without hell.

We must wake ourselves up! Or somebody else will take our place, and bear our cross, and thereby rob us of our crown.

God loves with a great love the man whose heart is bursting with a passion for the impossible.[17]

Prayer: Monica,
PRAYING MOTHER
(AD 332–387)

Many are within that army of heavy-hearted parents who lament over a prodigal son or daughter. And perhaps no pain is like that of a godly mother who, as hope burns low, can only weep, sigh—and pray. Time may pass, but that God-given maternal instinct never departs or diminishes, and the angst experienced in particular times of crisis because of their wanderer is like no other. Yet it is this godly sorrow which, at times, serves to wring out of a soul the deepest and purest prayer that can ascend to heaven. We so often feel that if only we could 'take the lid off the machine' and see the effects of our prayers, we might be encouraged to pray more often. If only we could draw back the earthly curtain to catch a glimpse of our prayers at work, we feel we would have more incentive to pray. But, alas, we are unable; 'we walk by faith and not by sight', and that is especially true when it comes to the exercise of prayer. Yet there is nothing more heartening than to hear of answers to prayer, and when we look at the life of one of the finest and most influential Christians with whom God has blessed our world—Augustine of Hippo— this former prodigal would later testify that, after God, he owed all to his mother, Monica, who cried out to God for him through all the years of his reckless and wayward life.

Hippo is the ancient name of a city in North Africa, and around the fourth century it was a centre of Christianity; it was from here that Augustine would exert his considerable influence. We will weave back and forth between Monica and Augustine's lives, in order to trace something of the way in which the burdened prayers of a mother restrained, and then, under the hand of God, brought home her straying prodigal safely into the Saviour's fold.

Monica

The mother of Augustine was born into a Christian home in Carthage (Tunisia) in North Africa, where she and her several sisters were cared for by an elderly maidservant who had previously also cared for their father when he was a child. She exercised greater influence than their earthly mother, and for good. The maidservant was known for her 'holy severity in administering correction' when bringing up the girls, and this was to prove of great use when Monica grew a little too fond of wine in her youth. After being taunted by a slave girl for being drunk, Monica felt a healthy shame and resolved not to drink from then on.

She married a pagan husband, Patricius, an ill-tempered, truculent man who was repeatedly unfaithful to her. It was this unhappiness that led Monica to embrace the comfort of the gospel, and then provided her with the incentive to love and respect her husband as if he were Christ. Augustine later wrote of his mother's quiet and gentle spirit, and of how she spoke of Christ to Patricius 'through her virtues' by which Christ made her beautiful. When Monica first married, her mother-in-law was quite hostile to her, but it would be Monica's joy and reward in later years to see both Patricius and his mother become Christians.

Birth and early signs of trouble

In AD 354, twenty-three-year-old Monica gave birth to a son while living in Tagaste, a small town in North Africa. The baby, Augustine, was a brother to Navigus and Perpetua. It soon became clear that he was a highly intelligent boy, but, like many lads in our day, he preferred playing games to studying. Difficult to motivate, he caused his parents concern quite early in life, and even the schoolmaster's whip was unable to persuade him to work, which he found tedious and sought to avoid by telling 'innumerable lies'. Patricius and Monica were determined to see their son succeed and, seeking to steer him to a career in the legal profession, they planned to send him to Carthage to study when he reached the age of seventeen. Because of the hefty expense of this, they were forced to withdraw him from school for a year prior to his leaving in order to raise the necessary finance. This would prove to be a costly decision morally, and would be a case of 'the devil finding work for idle hands'. In his classic work, the extraordinarily transparent *Confessions* which he wrote later in life, Augustine describes the life of debauchery from which he would be finally rescued, but points to this crunch year as the time when he set his feet firmly upon the path that led downwards to his wild and immoral lifestyle. 'The briers of unclean desires grew rank [putrid] over my head,' he wrote, 'and there was no hand to root them out.' His parents cared, and were deeply concerned—he later admits how his mother's words of warning pained him. But there was, at this point, no strong hand of redemption to deliver this passionate and excitable young man from the power of his sin.

ICE AND FIRE

Deeper into darkness

When this lamentable year passed, Augustine moved away from home to study, as so many young people do in our day. In Carthage, he applied himself well to his studies, but the cloud of financial concern hovered once more when his father died, leaving the continuance of his son's course in doubt. Romanius, a friend, having noted the abilities and potential of his companion, stepped in and financed the remainder of his studies there. But Augustine was being drawn deeper into sin and darkness, attending gambling dens, the racecourse and amphitheatre, and descending even further into moral decline and impurity. Commenting on this period of his life he admits, 'I was foul and dishonourable.' What struggles and sorrows exist within the heart of a prodigal that none know of but himself. 'Even in laughter the heart may ache' (Prov. 14:13). Others may throw themselves into a life of debauchery with minimal discomfort or conviction, but one brought up with God's Word cannot escape the light and power of it, no matter how entrenched they may be in sin.

When he was nineteen, Augustine became fascinated and then ensnared by a Gnostic-type heresy called Manichaeism, not unlike modern New Age thought. Monica was heartbroken when she learned of this, having prayed that the spiritual void he was experiencing might lead him to Christ. But now her son seemed even more distant and hopeless than ever. Sadly, she was without the comfort of knowing that her concern was like an arrow to her wayward son's heart through the dark nine years of his captivity to the heresy. Again, in his *Confessions* he wrote, 'My mother, Thy faithful one, wept to Thee for me, more than mothers weep the bodily deaths of their children . . . O Lord, Thou did not despise her tears, when streaming down, they watered the ground in every place where she prayed.'

Heavenly comfort

During this time, Augustine had a son with the woman he was living with. It seemed the more earnestly Monica prayed, the deeper her son became embedded in his dissolute lifestyle, and she may well have been tempted to despair had it not been for gracious encouragements from the faithful God who 'will not let you be tempted beyond what you can bear. But when you are tempted, he will also provide a way out so that you can endure it' (1 Cor. 10:13). To comfort her, Monica was given a dream in which she saw a shining young man approach her, joyful and smiling. He enquired why she was so sorrowful, and she replied by saying that it was because of the inevitable destruction of her son. When she looked up and saw the man's face, she saw that it was Augustine himself, who then told her, 'Where you are, there I will be also.' However, her joy on receiving this dream was soon to be dampened.

So spiritually hard and blind was her son that, when Monica repeated this dream to him, he perversely turned the meaning around, saying the dream only meant that 'You will become a Manichaean, like I am.' But she held on to that which she believed was an encouragement to her from God, praying on, and she refused to believe that her supplications would go unheeded and unanswered.

ICE AND FIRE

The struggle continues

For nine long years, Augustine continued this lifestyle, and the battle for his soul intensified, felt by both mother and son. The mother prayed on, totally unaware of the distress heaven was placing upon the prodigal's heart as he sank ever lower into sin. 'For almost nine years, I wallowed in the mire of that deep pit, and the darkness of falsehood . . . all which time, that chaste, godly widow, now more cheered with hope, yet not relaxing in her weeping and mourning, ceased not to bewail my case unto Thee.' Monica, seeking to employ any strategy and means to reach her son, knew that the local bishop was a man well acquainted with the Scriptures and might be willing to speak with him. But when she approached him, he decided that a conversation with him would be unwise because he considered Augustine unteachable, resistant and puffed up with his 'knowledge'. The bishop's wisdom brought an amount of relief and consolation to Monica who felt the pressure of wanting to 'do something'. Parents today may also find comfort from his wise words: 'Let him alone a while, only pray to God for him . . . Go thy ways and God bless thee, for it is not possible that the son of those tears should perish.'

The darkest hour before the dawn

Augustine had begun to lecture on the art of rhetoric. He was restless and had moved from Carthage back to his home town of Tagaste, and then on to Rome. Chinks in the armour of Manichaeism were becoming evident. Although living a life of debauchery, Augustine was seeking something higher and became disillusioned by the hypocritical lifestyles of a number of followers within the sect. By now, he was twenty-seven, and moving to Milan, he began to listen to, and be affected by, a well-known preacher, Ambrose, the bishop of that city. Meanwhile, he continued plummeting deeper into sin and hopelessness—and a battle was raging within. His now-famous cry was, 'Give me chastity, but not yet.' He ended the relationship with the mother of his child with whom he had lived for so long, and pursued a girl who was not yet of marriageable age. Whilst waiting for that time to arrive, Augustine entered into yet another illicit relationship. But, despite his apparent freefall into sin, he was now eagerly searching the Scriptures, and heavenly light was beginning to penetrate the darkness of his soul. 'How foul I was, how crooked and defiled,' he would write.

The struggle came to a head when he and a friend, Alypius, who shared accommodation with him, listened to a man who had surrendered all to follow Jesus Christ. Augustine, deeply agitated, turned to his friend, saying, 'What ails us, Alypius, are we ashamed to follow?' After uttering these words, he rushed out into the garden. Going to the farthest corner and throwing himself to the ground, he cried, 'How long, O Lord? Wilt Thou be angry with me for ever? Remember not our former iniquities.' Weeping bitterly, he heard between his sobs what seemed to be a child's voice saying over and over again, 'Take up and read. Take up and read.' Rising up, and sensing that this was not simply the voice of a child speaking, Augustine hurried back to the place where he had left the Scriptures. His eyes fell immediately upon the words 'not in carousing and drunkenness, not in sexual immorality and debauchery, not in dissension and jealousy. Rather, clothe yourselves with the Lord Jesus Christ, and do not think about

ICE AND FIRE

how to gratify the desires of the flesh' (Rom. 13:13–14). The miracle of grace had taken place. 'Instantly,' he tells us, 'by a light of serenity infused into my heart, all the darkness of doubt vanished away.' Alypius was also converted that same day, and the pair were later baptized together by Bishop Ambrose. Immediately, they rushed to see Monica to inform her. Having at times tasted the sorrows of hell, she now joyfully soared as she joined with those in heaven rejoicing over this sinner who had repented, this prodigal who once was dead but was now alive, who once was so lost but now was found.

The effects of prayer

'Our praying needs to be pressed and pursued with an energy that never tires, a persistency which will not be denied, and a courage that never fails,' wrote E. M. Bounds—no doubt an echo of our Lord's words that we ought 'always [to] pray and not give up' (Luke 18:1). There is no glory in prayer, and perhaps the most effectual prayer is, in fact, painful and pressed out of us through trying, unwelcome circumstances. But who can assess the extent to which prayer impacts our world? Through a mother's earnest prayers, Augustine went on to be one of the leading church fathers, a great defender of the faith, one of the most influential and important of our early theologians, and even considered by secular writers to be one of the pillars of Western civilization.

Augustine was now thirty-three years of age and Monica fifty-six, and neither had any idea that her life would soon be over, as she died of an illness not long after Augustine's conversion. She would never see her son's rise to prominence, but her work on earth was completed. Before her death, she said,

Son, for my own part I have no further delight in anything in this life. What I do here any longer, and to what end I am here, I know not, now that my hopes in this world are accomplished. One thing there was, for which I desired to linger for a while in this life, that I might see you a Christian before I died . . .

GEMS

Thou hast made us for Thyself, O Lord, and our heart is restless until it finds its rest in Thee.

For what am I to myself without Thee, but a guide to my own downfall?

Thou called and shouted and burst my deafness. Thou flashed, shone, and scattered my blindness. Thou breathed odours, and I drew in breath and panted for Thee. I tasted, and I hunger and thirst. Thou touched me, and I burned for Thy peace.

When I come to be united to Thee with all my being, then there will be no more pain and toil for me, and my life shall be a real life, being wholly filled by Thee.[18]

ICE AND FIRE

FAITH: CHARLES AND PRISCILLA STUDD,
FOOLS AND FANATICS
(1860–1931; 1864–1929)

'At God's command I left all that is usually thought to make life worth living . . . and have been called fool and fanatic again and again,' said the elderly man, with eyes that twinkled with good humour as they looked out from his leathery face. Not many of us are called to be pioneer missionaries as was C. T. Studd, but each and every follower of Jesus Christ has received the command to take up our cross and follow Him. We all have been summoned to live a life of faith, turning our backs upon the ever-seductive charms and demands of this world, and to store up treasure in heaven. 'We live by faith, not by sight' is our motto, because 'without faith it is impossible to please God' (2 Cor. 5:7; Heb. 11:6), and as obedient children we desire with all our hearts to please Him. Studd gladly gave up his inherited fortune, as well as a hugely successful career as an England cricketer, in order to make Christ known. It was no small thing to renounce celebrity status, to become an 'unknown', buried in the depths of China, India and then Africa. And his critics were many. To those who would accuse the old Etonian of being over-the-top in his zeal (even within the church), Charles would respond with unassailable logic, 'How could I spend the best years of my life in living for the honours of this world, when thousands of souls are perishing every day?' His was no dour, joyless service, but he sparkled with outrageous humour and lived a life of comedic daring and cheery challenge, as his audacious faith made an enormous impact upon the world which is felt to this day. The Worldwide Evangelization Crusade (WEC International) which he founded has a staff today of almost two thousand serving in eighty countries around the world.

Silver spoon in his mouth

Edward Studd was a retired indigo planter who, having made his fortune in India, returned to England to spend it. His three boys, Kynaston, George and Charles, lacked for nothing and were encouraged to be like their race-horse-owning father, who had a passion for riding and cricket, in particular. But all was to change for Edward after he went to hear a visiting American evangelist, D. L. Moody, who was causing quite a stir through his meetings held at London's Drury Lane Theatre. 'I'm going to hear him,' he announced. 'There must be some good about the man, or he would never be abused so much by the papers.' Edward was powerfully converted and his priorities turned upside down in an instant: he turned his back on the turf and from a life packed with empty pleasures to one of helping others to seek his Saviour.

Edward Studd lived only two years afterwards, but the impact upon the family was immediate—although not welcomed. The boys were all away schooling at Eton when they heard about their father, and they initially resisted his every attempt to interest them in the gospel. However, shortly afterwards, and unknown to each other at the time, all three were converted.

Although they all excelled at cricket, Charles stood out above them all, and his exceptional talent eventually gained him a place in the Cambridge and then England teams. Reckoning him the leading all-round player for England, the *Cricket Annual* wrote, 'Mr C. T. Studd must for the second year in succession be accorded the premier position as all-round cricketer.' He had become a national figure.

Crisis

In 1884, the twenty-four-year-old Charles, having graduated from Cambridge the previous year, was thrown into turmoil when his brother George was taken seriously ill and the wealthy young sportsman was confronted uncomfortably with eternal values. 'What is all the fame and flattery worth,' he reasoned, 'when a man comes to face eternity?' Since his conversion six years previously, he had drifted into 'an unhappy backslidden state', but he now arrived at this solemn conclusion: 'I know that cricket would not last, and honour would not last, and nothing in this world would last, but it was worthwhile living for the world to come.' From then onwards, Charles began witnessing to his friends and fellow players and he discovered that the joy experienced when sharing Christ eclipsed all others: 'I cannot tell you what joy it gave me to bring the first soul to the Lord Jesus Christ. I have tasted almost all the pleasures this world can give. Those pleasures were as nothing compared to the joy that the saving of that one soul gave me.'

The Cambridge Seven

The Holy Spirit had been stirring profoundly among the students at Cambridge University—it would not be too strong a word to call it a time of 'revival'. God had drawn not only Studd but a number of other bright young men to a place of surrender and all-out service. Charles had already applied and been accepted to join Hudson Taylor's China Inland Mission, but six others were to join him. Together, they would be known as the Cambridge Seven. After their acceptance into the China Inland Mission, the Seven toured England and Scotland, preaching, rousing and appealing to their listeners to follow Christ. Their influence was widely felt and became the catalyst for the formation of the Student Volunteer Movement and Inter-Varsity Fellowship. In February 1885, seven scholarly and athletic young men stood to testify how God had changed their lives and they were now offering themselves for mission work. Their testimonies were deeply moving and their words pointed and punchy:

What are we going to do? What is the use of great meetings like this if the outcome is not to be something worthy of the name of Jesus? He wants us to take up our cross and follow Him—to leave fathers, mothers, brothers, sisters, friends, property, and everything we hold dear, to carry the gospel to the perishing.

They left for China the following day.

China

So the group set sail for China and arrived in Shanghai on 18 March. They were given a gracious token on the journey in the form of leading the ship's captain to Christ. On arrival, they at once began study of the language, for seven to ten hours a day, and took to the wearing of Chinese clothes, as well as eating with, and like, the Chinese. In December of that year, Charles's twenty-fifth birthday arrived, and along with it a family inheritance of £29,000 (the estimated equivalent of over £2.5 million today), but already he had determined that it would go to the Lord's work. The fortune was divided up between the ministries of D. L. Moody, George Müller orphanages, George Holland's work among the poor in London's East End, the Salvation Army and China Inland Mission, leaving an amount in his own account which soon would be disposed of!

In 1887, an attractive Irish girl arrived in Shanghai, one of a party of new workers. With her blue eyes, golden hair and lively personality, Priscilla Livingstone Stewart had previously fitted in well with the partying crowd in Belfast, but had since been captured by the love of Christ and had set out for a life of adventure in service of Him. She received her 'baptism of fire' having joined the Salvation Army, and spoke glowingly of 'the old boots, wood, stones, rotten eggs and oranges thrown at us'. But the Irish lass had no idea at the time that this was just the right preparation for the love of her life. She began working in a sailors' home, where her future husband would preach, and where they saw the Spirit powerfully convicting and converting men from the Royal Navy, many from the depths of sin. The couple were instantly attracted to each other, but she was soon to move to central China, travelling alone by steamer up the Yangtze river, while Studd prepared to head north.

A real 'Hallelujah Lassie'

It was during this time of separation that warm, romantic letters were exchanged which led to their engagement. The confirmed bachelor's plans had been turned upside down, and he remembered how, on a previous occasion, he had remarked to his co-workers, 'I don't want to marry, but if I do, I want to marry a real Salvation Army Hallelujah Lassie.' Just after their commitment to each other, however, both were to have a brush with death. The well-known Chinese evangelist Pastor Shi had arrived at their mission station and agreed to hold an open-air meeting in that city, so Priscilla and four other girls, seeking to uphold the preacher in prayer, knelt in the snow and sleet. Many were affected not only by the message, but also by the sight of these earnest young women, and tears streamed down the faces of even Chinese men. But there was a price to pay, as Priscilla contracted pneumonia and became so seriously ill that they summoned her fiancé to come quickly to her. But he himself had been at death's door with pleurisy in both lungs, typhoid and then pneumonia. Amazingly, he recovered sufficiently to go to her, and the pair eventually both recuperated. Friends were impressed by their love and dedication, and all were agreed that they should marry without hesitation. 'It will be no easy life, no life of ease which I could offer you,' Charles cautioned his fiancée,

but one of toil and hardship . . . I just want to beseech you, darling, that we both make the same request every day to our Father, that we may give each other up to Jesus every single day of our lives, to be separated or not just as He pleases, that neither of us may ever make an idol of the other . . . I love you for your love for Jesus, I love you for your zeal towards Him, I love you for your faith in Him, I love you for your love for souls, I love you for loving me, I love you for your own self, I love you forever and ever. I love you because Jesus has used you to bless me and fire my soul. I love you because you will always be a red-hot poker making me run faster.

ICE AND FIRE

United to fight for Jesus

'Charlie' and 'Scilla', as they fondly called each other, married in March 1888, the bride wearing a long white sash emblazoned with the words 'United to fight for Jesus'. Both knelt and made the solemn vow to God, 'We will never hinder one another from serving Thee.' After the ceremony, the couple left immediately to open a new work in the inland city of Lungang-Fu. Just before the wedding, Charles had presented his bride-to-be with the considerable remainder of his inheritance. What were they to do with it? 'Charlie,' said Scilla, 'what did the Lord tell the rich young man to do? Sell all. Well then, we will start clear with the Lord at our wedding.' They were left with $5 and some bedding to last them the next forty-one years of their marriage. Studd was again motivated by logic not emotion, believing that God's purposes could be confirmed through providential circumstances, such as a sum of money being given at just the right moment. He encouraged Christians to take risks in Christian work, attempting what was beyond them and their resources, and trusting God to provide what they actually needed, not wanted. 'Funds are low again, Hallelujah,' he would later write. 'Perhaps we have been taking things too much for granted and the Lord wants to remind us out of whose hand we are fed.'

Danger and hardship

Their remaining time in China was to be marked by the typical New Testament paradoxes of joy and sorrow, battle and blessing. They would see growth in God's family and in their own. For five years, 1888–1892, they couldn't leave their house without a bombardment of curses from their neighbours. Charles spent a good deal of time at an opium refuge for the victims of the drug, and during seven years around 800 people went through the refuge, some converted to Christ as well as cured of their addiction. Their first child was born in 1889, when Scilla had a relapse and almost died. Four more children were to follow, the fifth living just one day. The four children who lived were girls: Grace, Dorothy, Edith and Pauline. A sixth child was born after their return to England, a boy, but he lived only two days. Charles was delighted with his girls: 'One of the curses of China is not to let their little girls live . . . God gave me four little girls, He gave them to me for a purpose. We wanted them [the Chinese] to learn that God loves little girls as well as little boys.'

In 1894, after ten years of service in China, they felt sure God was leading them to return to England, a move made easier due to the fact that Charles's asthmatic condition had worsened. The separation was difficult, as many were attached to them, with even Chinese men sobbing their hearts out as they departed, never to meet again in this world.

America

During this period, Charles was kept fully occupied, speaking both in England and also in the USA, where, having heard of 'the Cambridge Seven', they had given an invitation to the former celebrated sportsman to visit. A flame was burning there. He stayed for eighteen demanding months, speaking as many as six times a day, and seldom less than an hour each time, with hundreds coming and offering themselves for service. The missionary didn't mince his words. To one who informed Charles that he was quite happy with his spiritual state, he shot back, 'Then you are quite sure to be damned!' But then he went on to explain the futility of trying to live up to God's standard by his own efforts, and the need for God's grace through Christ alone. In 1897, he returned to England for three years, which gave him time to recuperate and to seek God in readiness for the next mission, which was to be in India, being mindful of his father's dying wish that the gospel be taken there.

India

Although India was a better climate for him, Charles's asthma problem continued to plague him, as he hardly slept, sitting up in a chair night after night, fighting for breath. Studd's chief work in India was as a pastor. With Scilla alongside him, they served the Union Church at Ootacamund in south India, a church that reached out to all kinds of people with the gospel. A week never passed without one to three conversions. During this time, all four daughters came to trust Christ and were baptized before the family's return to England in 1906. For two years, the fiery missionary spoke to what must have amounted to tens of thousands of men— many totally unchurched—who were drawn to hear him because of his sporting reputation, a good number of whom came to Christ. All this was worthwhile work, but there was an indescribable churning deep within. As yet, he still felt as though he had not arrived at his life's work, and he would later express that stirring eloquently: 'Some want to live within the sound of church or chapel bell; I want to run a rescue shop, within a yard of hell.'

Needy cannibals

Waiting time is never wasted time, and God's ways and timings are always impeccable. One day in 1908, while walking in Liverpool, an unusual sign caught Charles's eyes: 'Cannibals want missionaries.' The sign had been placed by a Dr Karl Chum, who was burdened for reaching the as-yet unevangelized Nile-to-Niger region of central Africa. Studd was stirred, but he faced enormous obstacles. He was no longer a young man, he was penniless, his health was poor, he had already been warned by the doctor, he had been dropped by a committee and he would need to leave behind his wife and children. Priscilla, who was suffering with asthma and a heart condition, pleaded with him not to go, as did his mother also, but nothing and no one could deter him. Despite heartbreak, fears and concerns, he again resorted to holy logic when justifying his actions:

Last June at the mouth of the Congo there awaited a thousand prospectors, traders, merchants and gold seekers, waiting to rush into these regions as soon as the government opened the door to them, for rumour declared that there is an abundance of gold. If such men hear so loudly the call of gold and obey it, can it be that the ears of Christ's soldiers are deaf to the call of God? Are gamblers for gold so many, and gamblers for God so few?

Charles informed the committee: 'Gentlemen, God has called me, and I will go. I will blaze a trail, though my grave may only become a stepping stone that younger men may follow.' The call was too great to resist, so on 15 December 1910, at the age of fifty, the pioneer sailed alone to embark upon his greatest work. He would eventually prove the doctors wrong,

staying in Africa eighteen years, and would see revival far
beyond anyone's expectations.

Crazy faith

Trekking through dangerous territory in the Congo one
day, Studd and his party found themselves without food or
money. But he walked by faith and not by sight, and, aided
by his daring humour, joked, 'Why do breeches have so
many buttons? To be cut off and used as money in Central
Africa, of course.' Returning home in 1914, Charlie found his
beloved Priscilla very ill, but still faithfully carrying on their
HQ responsibilities. She was the anchor and mainstay of the
work, faithfully forming prayer centres, issuing monthly
brochures by the thousand, writing up to thirty letters a
day, and designing and editing the mission magazine. Studd
admitted that he found he was able to issue his stirring appeals
more effectively through their widely delivered publication
than face-to-face. Sadly, all too often, the wives, children and
families of missionaries, pastors and evangelists can be left
in the shadows, despite the sacrifices they, too, are called to
make. But nothing is missed by our all-seeing Father, who
will ensure that not even a cup of cold water given in His
name will go unrewarded.

The time came for Charlie to return to Africa, so a farewell
rally was fixed for 14 July, with the actual departure on 24 July
1916. This would be the third time he had to leave his wife,
which they found increasingly difficult as the years went by.
When returning to the field from his previous visit home, he
had written a poignant letter to Scilla from on board the ship:
'I shall ever picture you running with the camera. I longed, but

dare not say "good-bye" or kiss again.' Now came another parting, and they would see each other for only two weeks during his remaining fifteen years in Africa. A young man at one of his meetings in England chided the elderly missionary for leaving behind his family at his age. But Charles replied, 'If Jesus Christ be God and died for me, then no sacrifice can be too great for me to make for Him.' The day after he left, something remarkable occurred. Priscilla got up from her invalid's bed, never to return. She began to live a tornado-type life, travelling the globe on behalf of her husband and the mission, touring the USA, Canada, Australia, New Zealand and South Africa, and she was rated as one of the world's finest missionary speakers.

Only one life . . .

The impact of the gospel work in the Congo was great, as they witnessed 'ignorant, semi-naked and desperately depraved creatures' become beautiful new creations, rejoicing in the Jesus who had loved and saved them. As the number of converts increased, mission stations were built, and other missionaries went out to join Charles, including his son-in-law, Norman Grubb, who united with him in the painstaking yet essential task of translating the Scriptures. He would eventually succeed his father-in-law in leading the Heart of Africa Mission, which eventually would become the Worldwide Evangelization Crusade. Studd plodded on, despite his asthma, recurring malaria, dysentery, chills, toothache and pain of gallstones that were ever with him, yet he continued working from eight to as many as eighteen hours a day.

Tragically, his ill-health caused him to turn to morphine for relief, finally causing him to become addicted. For many at home, this was the final straw, and the mission's committee felt compelled to remove him from the very mission which he had founded. Priscilla made a short visit to the Congo to see him, but that was their final meeting, and his beloved Irish bride died the following year, in 1929. Her Charlie was soon to join her. On Sunday, 12 July 1931, after conducting a five-hour meeting at Ibambi, he was taken ill with a fever, which worsened over the following days. And on 16 July, the old campaigner used the little breath he had to gasp in victory, 'Hallelujah! Hallelujah!'

So passed a man with a character large enough for his faults to be plainly visible. But with all his flaws and foibles, Charles Thomas Studd was a man who simply took Jesus at His word, seeking to live by faith, and as a result, was one whom God could abundantly bless. Highly quotable, Studd continues to be remembered best of all perhaps for two lines which have adorned many a wall or refrigerator door over the years:

Only one life 'twill soon be past.
Only what's done for Christ will last.

GEMS

Difficulties, dangers, disease, death, or divisions don't deter any but Chocolate Soldiers from executing God's will.

True religion is like the smallpox. If you get it, you give it to others and it spreads.

ICE AND FIRE

A man is not known by his effervescence but by the amount of real suffering he can stand.

We are frittering away time and money in a multiplicity of conferences, conventions and retreats, when the real need is to go straight and full steam into battle . . .[19]

WEAKNESS: LILIAS TROTTER,
THE FRAIL PIONEER
(1853–1928)

'If God wanted weakness and foolishness, He had it,' wrote the sensitive, creative young woman who turned down the prospect of a brilliant career as an artist in order to venture into dangerous uncharted Muslim regions to tell them about Jesus Christ.

Cocooned?

Isabella Lilias Trotter was born on 14 July 1853 into an affluent home in Marylebone, London, enjoying the kind of comfortable upbringing that might possibly have ruined her for any demanding future work. Alexander Trotter was a wealthy stockbroker who, after the death of his first wife (with whom he had six children), married Lilias's mother, Isabella. Lilias was the eldest of three children born to them. The atmosphere in their typically Victorian home was godly, disciplined and loving. The family lived just a short distance—but a million miles—away from the squalor and distress of the East End where William Booth was gallantly labouring, yet Alexander was a kind and gentle man who was thoughtful and generous in respect to the poor. The children were taught at home by a governess and Lilias became proficient in languages, drawing and singing. She especially enjoyed the holidays, ice skating and tobogganing in winter and then romping in the leafy glades of Epping Forest during summer months. But although, in one sense, Lilias was cocooned from hardship, she would not escape life's sorrows, and when she was twelve her father died of an illness. Her heart was broken, and she felt there was nothing left to live for. It was at this time of grief and blankness that she came to cast herself upon the love of the Father who never leaves us, and she discovered in Him the depth of beauty she had longed for when her artistic eyes observed and her sensitive spirit admired nature.

The years passed, and when aged nineteen, Lilias attended with her mother a Higher Life Conference, which was the forerunner of the Keswick Conferences, which she would later attend regularly and whose support she would enjoy in her ministry. God undoubtedly deepened her faith and experience at this time. She wrote,

A path lies within our reach, that makes the ordinary Christian life look cold and colourless by contrast . . . It is to many of us a distinctly fresh life when God's Spirit leads us to the objective side, lifting our gaze from the road beneath our feet to the form of Him who goes before, and riveting it there by His radiant beauty.

Her eyes, however, were opened not only to the loveliness of Jesus Christ, but also to the dire needs in the world around her. These were days when strong forces for good were at work among God's people. As the church began to enjoy new depths in devotion to Christ, a sense of the church militant was being grasped once more and Christians were rising to meet the challenge of action, both at home and overseas.

Torn

Lilias was also impacted by the visit of D. L. Moody, who was conducting meetings in London at this time, even receiving training from Moody himself on how to help people who were seeking and enquiring after God. She launched herself into working with various local mission outreaches, gaining valuable experience in what we would today call urban mission. But another hunger was stirring within this passionate young woman. In 1876, aged twenty-three, Lilias travelled to Europe with her mother and sister. The majestic beauty of the snowy Alps reduced her to tears and inspired her to capture something of the wonder in her sketches. Whilst in Venice, the famous artist, critic, writer and philosopher John Ruskin happened to be staying at the same hotel. As mothers often do, her mother sought to make the talents of her daughter known, and sent Ruskin—the leading art expert of the day—a folder of Lilias's watercolours. He was later to say how irritating he found this, but, to his surprise, although aware that the young artist had received no formal training, he found the watercolours 'an extremely right-minded and careful work'.

He was impressed—so much so that he decided to take Lilias under his wing, tutoring her in preparation to become what he considered her capable of: a world-class artist. The two paths on which she was walking could not have been farther apart: on one day, making a trip with her sister to meet with the eminent Ruskin in his Lake District home, immersed in colour and culture; and almost the next, visiting the dark, depressing sights of the most deprived and depraved areas of London. Ruskin found himself becoming increasingly agitated by his protégée's 'distraction', feeling that she was spending too much time on the streets of London. He plainly set before her the choice she had to make. If she was willing to give herself wholly to art, 'she would be the greatest living painter and do things that would be immortal'.

Although it was an agonizing choice to make, Lilias realized that she could not serve two masters, and that only one passion must consume her. Ruskin was not only devastated by her decision, but utterly baffled that such talent could be squandered, cast aside in order to rescue immoral women from the street. He expressed not only his bewilderment but perhaps another motive when writing,

Am I not bad enough?
Am I not good enough?
Am I not whatever it is enough, to be looked after a little when I am ill, as well as those little Magdalenes?

Inner city, outer weakness

For the next ten years, the tall, slender young woman with light brown hair and sensitive mouth would be found working among prostitutes and 'lost girls' in Central London with the YWCA. 'Why this waste?' was the attitude of many friends. By taking this path, she was, in fact, choosing also a life of singleness, as Victorian England was very much divided and influenced by class. No desirable young woman would be found working in such a degrading environment, and mothers of the class to which Lilias belonged would never wish their sons to take on such a 'challenge'. She demonstrated immense courage and compassion as she negotiated the dark streets in order to bring the street-walkers back to the hostel for a night's sleep, respite and, hopefully, rescue when introduced to the Good Shepherd. In 1884, when just into her thirties, Lilias had to undergo minor surgery, but the effects were to be significant. So exhausted was she beforehand that her time of recovery was prolonged, and it was discovered that she had been left with a permanently damaged heart. Even though feeling distinctly weakened, she continued working. But she was getting nearer to what God wanted her to be, and unknown to her, change was on the way.

Lilias made the acquaintance of two women whose influence upon her would change the direction and sphere of her labours for the next forty or so years. It was the Christlikeness of the lives of Adeline Braithwaite and Lelie Duff that first caught her attention. 'I do not remember that they said anything to me personally about it but . . . they were all aglow, I saw that they had a fellowship with Jesus that I knew nothing about, so I began to pray, "Lord, give me the fellowship with Thee over the heathen that Thou hast given these two."' The answer to her prayer was not long delayed, and she recorded, 'Not many weeks later it began to come; a strange, yearning love for those who were in the land of the shadow of death—a feeling that Jesus could speak to me about them and that I could speak to Him . . . '

A voice calling

Neither of her two friends were called to serve overseas among 'the heathen', but their concern for the lost there would be used of God to send others. One of these would be Lilias Trotter, and as she prayed for God's work overseas and uttered the words 'North Africa', a deep stirring in her soul was felt, 'as though a voice were calling her', she said. But how could she possibly leave behind her invalid sister whom she was committed to caring for six months each year? God would not have us in doubt regarding His call, however, and in May 1887 she was at a meeting where the missionary speaker began by saying that he had just returned from Algeria in North Africa. 'In that first sentence,' she said, 'God's call had sounded; if Algeria was so near as that, I could spend half the year there, and the other half at home.' On her thirty-fourth birthday, 14 July 1887, she sent her application to the North Africa Mission, but was distraught to learn that she failed their health examination, due to concern about her weak heart. They consented to her working 'in harmony with this mission, but not connected to it'.

Anyone else might have been deterred by this, but not this frail pioneer: she decided that she would go independently.

Algeria

On 5 March 1888, Lilias, accompanied by her two friends Blanche Haworth and Katie Stuart, was given a rousing send-off at Waterloo station as their friends and supporters sang 'Crown Him Lord of All'. There was no doubting the weakness and fear they felt, but, having a carriage to themselves, the ladies knelt and placed all into the hands of the One who had called them and who is faithful. They travelled by train to Marseille and then by ship to Algiers, arriving on 9 March.

But where does one begin in a land where all is so strange and where their presence would hardly be welcomed? Much change had taken place in North Africa since the significant and extensive ministry of Augustine of Hippo fifteen hundred years previously. The ravaging Vandals had filled the vacuum left after the Roman Empire disintegrated, and that was then followed by the Byzantine Empire. But real spiritual change took place when Islam was brought to the area by Arabs from the East, and by 1830, when the French gained control, there was no sign of the once-vibrant Christian church. The Arabic language, culture and religion dominated and was strongly resistant to any change.

In a letter home, we see Lilias expressing not only the utter foolishness of their venture, humanly speaking, but also the breathtaking depth of their faith in God:

Not one of us would have been passed by a doctor for any missionary society. We did not know a soul in the place, nor a sentence in Arabic; nor did we have a clue as to how to begin work on untouched ground. We only knew we had to come. If God needed weakness, He had it! We were on a fool's errand . . . but the Moslem world that has challenged Christ for over twelve centuries has not had His last word yet.

They faced exactly the same challenge that we face today, seeing men and women, so many of them earnest and sincere, but snared by the very same hopeless system. But the God and Father of our Lord Jesus Christ reigns, and is our God.

Early years of ministry

In Algiers, the new missionaries rented a large fortress-like house, and their early years were undoubtedly their most difficult, having to face hostility and suspicion, not only from neighbours, but also from the authorities, all stemming from the inbred hostility of Islam for Christ and the gospel. Good-humouredly, they named their front door 'the door of a thousand dents' because of the treatment it received. Their first task was to learn Arabic, hiring a professional to help them. They longed to be able to communicate and felt the frustration of the language barrier, but they made contact with French-speaking locals, whom they would invite to the regular Sunday meetings the women held in their home. With the little Arabic they knew, they would write small portions of Scripture on card, and would sometimes ask the waiters in cafes they visited to read them aloud to all the customers. From the beginning, Lilias felt a special calling to reach the women, but this proved difficult because they remained in their homes, isolated from regular life. An Arab woman belonged to her father until marriage, and was then transferred to her husband, so, after serving one, she would be required to serve the other. From around the age of ten, a girl was veiled and cut off from all contact with other men. The only possible way—and things have not changed even up to today—was if another woman could be invited to the home, and children were often the key to this. Lilias would later write that the early years were like 'knocking our heads against stone walls'.

Dark and oppressive

It is hard for us to imagine how oppressive the atmosphere was for the pioneers, especially when they ventured, and then, in time, moved, into the Arabic quarter—an 'evil-smelling labyrinth of narrow alleys behind the port'. They were driven to the throne of grace, convinced that without divine aid, the satanic forces were too great for a handful of helpless novices. We glimpse the oppression that was felt in Lilias's own words: 'More than ever . . . we have sights of the deliberate power of the devil around us . . . the very air seems impregnated with devilry, and that sense of knowing him as the adversary has been keener than ever before.' But, gradually, over those early years, doors began to open, as gifts of tiny toys, sweets or basic medical remedies were shared. Hungry hearts were detected: 'Oh, Long One,' called out a veiled lady through a crack in the door, 'come and see me.' Now and then a glimpse of encouragement was received. They understood the words of one lady, who murmured in French, 'No one ever loved us like this before.' Sadly, at times, because of the sheer presence and pressure of sin and evil in which they lived, new converts would be drawn back, banished, beaten, even having their food or drink laced with drugs, opening the new believers to the surrounding evil influences. All too often, this would lead to the premature deaths of the converts, which the heavy-hearted ladies actually drew comfort from, resting in the belief that God was taking His lambs home in order to spare them.

After seven years, Lilias was forced to return to England for rest, due to her heart and nerves being worn by strain and stress, the extreme heat also proving most debilitating and exacerbating her condition. This would be a recurring pattern for this frail servant of God, as throughout her years of service she could only continue in the work by taking spells of rest and recuperation. Again, we are reminded that there is no 'wasted time' for the one whose heart and will is set on pleasing God. As well as having her batteries recharged, it was during these periods that much of her creative and evangelistic writing was produced. Lilias's journals were a combination of writings, paintings and sketches, with her devotional books providing a window into life in North

Africa for thousands living far away who knew nothing of the area. God had harnessed her gifts for a higher cause than the one John Ruskin had in mind.

Faith and perseverance

In her own words, this fragile servant of God clearly revealed that her ability to endure serving Christ in North Africa throughout four challenging decades was due to 'the stretched-out hand of faith on earth, acting in union with the stretched-out hand of God's power in heaven'.

Lilias was grieved by the unbelief that she would sometimes find in those who felt threatened by the grip and power of Islam. When attending a conference in Europe she talked with a man who referred to Muslims as 'a doomed race'. 'A doomed race!' she exclaimed. 'It does not sound very like "The God of Hope" or "The God of Love". A doomed creed is nearer the mark; the husk that imprisons the seed is doomed, that is all. Hallelujah!' She was indefatigable, and laboured on to win the Muslim world with a heart filled with faith and overflowing love. As well as producing far-reaching evangelistic materials, together with her faithful colleagues she was responsible for the founding of the Algiers Mission Band which she would, in her lifetime, see grow to include twenty-nine workers, with mission stations in at least fourteen desert towns. (AMB would later merge with North Africa Mission, which changed its name to Arab World Ministries.) Driven on by yearning love and compassion, she would at times go on reconnaissance trips on camel, visiting areas never before visited by a European woman. Lilias left behind a body of devotional literature, most notably, *Parable of the Cross* and *Parables of the Christ-Life*.

The gate of heaven

During her final three years, her heart condition confined Lilias to her bed and necessitated transferring the leadership responsibility of the Algiers Mission Band to others. She continued writing and, of course, her intercession for the North African peoples she loved. As she drew nearer to death, a friend described her as moving 'closer to the gate of heaven'. She remarked, 'Almost it seemed in the last year of her life . . . so strangely beautiful was the shining of spiritual light in a frail and outwearied body.'

On 27 August 1928, her friends gathered around her, and whilst they sang 'Jesus, Lover of My Soul', Lilias looked out of the window and exclaimed, 'A chariot and six horses!'

A friend asked her, 'You are seeing beautiful things?'

'Yes, many beautiful things.' She then lifted her hands in prayer, and, almost immediately, calmly drew her last breath.

Like many a life invested in the world to come, Lilias did not see the fruit of her prayers and labours that she longed for, in multitudes of Muslims turning to Christ. The ground was hard then, as it remains today, but we need to learn and relearn the value of one precious eternal soul in God's sight. Eternity shall reveal that '[our] labour in the Lord is not in vain' (1 Cor. 15:58). So we wait for the day when we shall be among that 'great multitude that no one [can] count, from every nation, tribe, people and language, standing before the throne and before the Lamb' (Rev. 7:9).

But I wonder how many of us there are who, because of

felt weakness, shyness, lack of confidence or, quite frankly, unbelief, are like Moses, who, when commissioned by God, looked around for someone else to do the job. At such times, we forget that God delights in weakness because it produces greater dependence upon Him—His power, His wisdom, His strength, His provision, and all to His glory.

GEMS

The result, small as it is, is worth all the years of work.

The crown of it was the revelation of the way that God can use weakness.

Take the very hardest thing in your life—the place of difficulty, outward or inward, and expect God to triumph gloriously in that very spot. Just there He can bring your soul into blossom.

I am seeing more and more that we begin to learn what it is to walk by faith when we learn to spread out all that is against us— all our physical weakness, loss of mental power, spiritual inability—all that is against us, inwardly and outwardly, as sails to the wind, and expect them to be vehicles for the power of Christ to rest upon us . . .[20]

Notes

1 Peter Masters, 'Foreword', in S. Pearce Carey, *William Carey* (London: Wakeman Trust, 1993), p. x.

2 John Piper, 'Holy Faith, Worthy Gospel, World Vision', Desiring God, 6 February 2007, https://www.desiringgod.org/messages/holy-faith-worthy-gospel-world-vision.

3 Sources: Paul Pease, *William Carey: The Missionary to India Who Attempted Great Things for God* (Leominster: Day One, 2005); Pearce Carey, *William Carey*; Fred Barlow, 'William Carey', in *Profiles in Evangelism* (Murfreesboro, TN: Sword of the Lord, 1976); Kellsye M. Finnie, *William Carey: By Trade a Cobbler* (Eastbourne: Kingsway, 1986).

4 Robert L. Peterson and Alexander Strauch, *Agape Leadership: Lessons from the Life of R. C. Chapman* (Colarado Springs: Lewis & Roth, 1991; Kindle edn), loc. 380.

5 Sources: Peterson and Strauch, *Agape Leadership*; E. F. and L. Harvey and E. Hey, 'Robert Cleaver Chapman', in *They Knew Their God* (Stoke-on-Trent: M.O.V.E. Press, 1980).

6 Sources: Robert Foster, *The Navigator* (Colorado Springs: NavPress, 1983); Betty Lee Skinner, *Daws: The Story of Dawson Trotman, Founder of the Navigators* (Grand Rapids: Zondervan, 1974).

7 In 1911 two young men from Ireland, Frederick and Arthur Wood, started a movement that would be used by God to bring the gospel to thousands of young people and to bless many Christian works in the UK and abroad. The movement became known as the National Young Life Campaign, and it had one aim: youth evangelism. Now simply called Young Life, hundreds of young people each year take part in beach missions (under the banner of United Beach Missions) and other forms of outreach in the UK and Europe.

8 Sources: Phyllis Thompson, *A London Sparrow* (London: Pan Books, 1972); Christine Hunter, *The Little Woman* (Chicago: Moody, 1970); Gladys Aylward, 'Testimony', Sermon Index, http://www.sermonindex.net/modules/mydownloads/viewcat.php?cid=63.

9 As Michael Reeves calls him in Michael Reeves, *The Unquenchable Flame* (Nottingham: IVP, 2009), p. 35.

10 Sources: Reeves, *Unquenchable Flame*; Michael Reeves and Tim Chester, *Why the Reformation Still Matters* (London: IVP, 2016); Steven Lawson, 'Fortress for Truth: Martin Luther', Ligonier Ministries, 5 October 2018, https://www.ligonier.org/blog/fortress-truth-martin-luther/.

11 Sources: Frank L. Houghton, *Amy Carmichael of Dohnavur* (Fort Washington, PA: CLC, 1996); Amy Carmichael, *Fragments That Remain* (London: SPCK, 1987).

12 Michael Hyatt, based on Corrie ten Boom's poem 'The Tapestry', *Michael Hyatt* (blog), 26 April 2012, https://michaelhyatt.com/how-your-life-is-like-a-tapestry/.

13 Sources: J. H. Merle d'Aubigné, *The Reformation in England*, Vol. 1 (Edinburgh: Banner of Truth, 1977); Reeves, *Unquenchable Flame*; Steven Lawson, 'Prince of Translators: William Tyndale', Ligonier Ministries, 25 September 2017, https://www.ligonier.org/blog/prince-translators-william-tyndale/.

14 Sources: F. W. Bourne, *Billy Bray: The King's Son* (Letchworth: Epworth Press, 1972); Fred M. Barlow, *Profiles in Evangelism* (Murfreesboro, TN: Sword of the Lord, 1976); 'Billy Bray, Enthusiastic Christian', *Herald of Grace*, https://heraldofgrace.org/billy-bray-enthusiastic-christian/.

15 Not to be confused with the UK organization of the same name (see note 7 above), Young Life is a parachurch ministry started in Dallas, Texas, in 1941 by Presbyterian minister Jim Rayburn, initially to suburban high school students. Young Life operates globally as several different organizations with different focuses. There are around 700 Young Life Club chapters worldwide.

16 Sources: Joni Eareckson Tada, *Joni* (Grand Rapids: Zondervan, 2001); Joni Eareckson Tada, *A Place of Healing* (Colorado Springs: David C Cook, 2016); Joni Eareckson Tada and Ken Tada, *Joni and Ken: An Untold Love Story* (Grand Rapids: Zondervan, 2013); Lausanne Committee for World Evangelization, 'Hidden and Forgotten People: Ministry among People with Disabilities', Lausanne Occasional Paper no. 35B, written principally by Joni Eareckson Tada and Jack S. Oppenhuizen (2005).

17 Sources: Harold Begbie, *The Life of William Booth*, 2 vols (London: Macmillan & Co., 1920; Kindle edn); Jim Winter, *Travel with William Booth*

(Epsom: Day One, 2003); Richard Collier Collins, *The General Next to God* (London: Fontana, 1968).

18 Sources: Augustine, *Confessions*, trans. E. B. Pewsey (London: Dent & Sons, 1975); Faith Cook, *Singing in the Fire* (Edinburgh: Banner of Truth, 1999).

19 Sources: Norman Grubb, *C. T. Studd* (Guildford: Lutterworth Press, 1978); Jean Walker, *Fool and Fanatic? Quotations from the Letters of C. T. Studd* (Gerrards Cross: WEC, 1980); Eileen Vincent, *C. T. Studd and Priscilla* (Eastbourne: Kingsway, 1988).

20 Sources: Patricia St John, *Until Morning Breaks* (Bromley: OM Publishing, 1990); Noel Piper, *Faithful Women and Their Extraordinary God* (Wheaton, IL: Crossway, 2005); E. F. and L. Harvey and E. Hey, *They Knew Their God* (Stoke-on-Trent: M.O.V.E. Press, 1980).

Epilogue: Keep the fire burning!

. . . and the fire must be kept burning on the altar. (Lev. 6:9)

I want you young men always to bear in mind that it is the nature of fire to go out; you must keep it stirred and fed, and the ashes removed. (William Booth)

John the Baptist is dead. The apostles are dead. Our heroes of centuries past are all dead. Like it or not, we are God's people for this hour; He has no one else. But Jesus is alive, His Spirit lives and is at work within us, and the God who strengthened, sustained and used the heroes of the faith throughout their days of storm, trial and battle remains unchanged. It has been rightly said, 'The history of the church has never been about great men and women of God. It has always been about the great God of men and women.'[1] In our day, we are not lacking in resources to equip us for the fight of faith, whether that is Bible teaching, literature, conferences, or any other tool needed for the job; in fact, we have benefits and advantages in our technological age that previous generations could only dream of. But surely our greatest need is for something of the holy flame and desire that blazed within the hearts of the saints we have just considered, and a host of others like them, which enabled them to live lives that were far beyond their natural ability.

SACRIFICE AND FIRE

Their stories speak of both sacrifice and fire. But they would have been the first to admit that they were totally reliant, above all else, on that which God Himself had provided through the sacrifice of Jesus Christ, and the equipping of the Holy Spirit. Calvary and Pentecost are unique past events, but we are called to appropriate the cleansing and power that flow from them both for living today. God is always the God of the 'now', and we dare not reek of the past, carrying with us in the twenty-first century the mothball stench of a stale faith which speaks of a God consigned to a museum. We draw upon the past for the sole reason of serving God and impacting the world in the 'now'.

In the tabernacle, according to the regulations for the burnt offering, the offering was not to be taken from the altar until it had been completely consumed by the fire: 'the fire must be kept burning on the altar' (Lev. 6:9). *John Calvin* commented,

The intent of this perpetuity was, that the offerings should be burnt with heavenly fire; for on the day that Aaron was consecrated, the sacrifice was reduced to ashes not by human means but miraculously, in token of approbation. True that God did not choose daily to exert this power; but He interposed the hand and labour of men in such a manner that the origin of the sacred fire should still be from heaven.[2]

All pointed, of course, to the coming One who would fulfil every Old Testament type and shadow. We trust in the perfect sacrifice of our Lord Jesus Christ for sin, and look to God to provide us with the sacred fire within by His Spirit. We need not only pardon, but also power from on high in order to live as God desires. It is all too easy to drift to a place where we are no longer sensitive to the One who dwells within, as *Matthew Henry* wrote, applying Leviticus 6:9: 'We must not only not quench the Spirit, but we must stir up the gift that is in us.'[3] It is our duty, in William Booth's words, to keep the fire 'stirred and fed, and the ashes removed'.

WEAK ENOUGH?

When reading Christian biography, one is struck by the sheer diversity of the men and women God can use, many of whom we perhaps would have passed over, or even written off. Some, of course, are out-and-out quirky and would no doubt be filed under the category of 'God's Irregulars'. But then, every one of us without exception is a victim, to a greater or lesser degree, of our genes, upbringing and circumstances, which perhaps begs the question, 'Who or what is normal?' If there is one silver thread that runs through the lives of the saints we have considered, it is their utter dependence upon God. Could it be that the ominous storm clouds gathering above our heads today are harbingers of blessing to come?

Ye fearful saints, fresh courage take;
The clouds you so much dread
Are big with mercy, and shall break
In blessings on your head.
             (William Cowper, 'God Moves in a Mysterious Way')

Perhaps, like some we read about, we shall be forced into a place of weakness in order that we might cry out for God to strongly enter the battle on our behalf. In these challenging days we should certainly not lack innovation or neglect seeking new ways and means to reach our generation. But the searching question is, are we doing this at the expense of admitting that without God we can do nothing? In other words, are our prayers those effectual cries of desperation that bring heaven down, or are they the casual accompaniment to our flesh-driven efforts? Overseas Missionary Fellowship veteran *Arthur Matthews*, in his powerful book (of over thirty years ago) *Born for Battle*, writes, 'In a day when new and exciting cutting edges are being recommended, the tendency is to be carried away with new ideas and relegate trusty weapons to a place of lesser significance or to throw them away altogether.' Then he adds pointedly, 'We need to realize that God is not going to use any means of operation just because it is innovative.'[4] We know only too well that God delights to bless those who cry out to him. The question is, are we humble enough, empty enough, desperate enough? Godly Methodist *Samuel Chadwick* (1860–1932) said, 'The soul's safety is in its heat . . . the Church is powerless without the Fire of the Holy Ghost. Destitute of Fire, nothing else counts; possessing Fire, nothing else really matters.'[5]

THE BLESSING OF PRESSURE

Whilst losing the freedom to evangelize and to practise our faith are the last things we would wish for—though we are only too aware that the screw is tightening—could this be the answer to the prayers of many over countless years for a reviving of the church? *Andrea Williams* is the winsomely spirited Director of Christian Concern, an organization at the forefront of the battle in the UK as they seek to represent Christians in the law courts and before the media. She reports how she went 'worn down by the woes of our nation' to a service of dedication to mark the translation of the Bible into modern Persian, and was greatly lifted in her spirit as she listened to the testimony of the Iranian believers at the meeting:

Oh what delight! And what joy in their singing as they praised Jesus! Then I was awestruck by their stories. Christians in Iran are paying a high price for their faith in Jesus. They have lost jobs, homes and even custody of children. Some have been physically abused. Hundreds are rejected by friends and family. And some are unjustly detained in Iran's notorious prison system. There are many martyrs and everyone in that room on Monday knew a martyr. Iranians are killed or imprisoned on false political charges relating to their Christian faith; usually they are convicted of 'undermining national security' through attending or organizing house church meetings, or sharing their faith.[6]

What was it that so encouraged Andrea? Receiving news of the deaths of God's people? No, it was the powerful reminder that nothing could rob Christians of their joy; that no power—human or demonic—can prevent Christ from building His church; and that persecution and blessing are so often wed together as one.

ALL'S WELL THAT ENDS WELL

What a difference it makes when we know that a story has a happy ending, and Christians are in no doubt concerning the outcome of the cosmic battle that currently rages. In the book of Revelation, John the apostle has the curtain pulled back, enabling him to see the end of all things: that even though he is in exile for his faith, and the mighty Roman Empire seems to have the upper hand, it is just for a short season of time. He was shown things that 'must soon take place' (Rev. 1:1) and transported to see sights and hear sounds that would bring comfort to him in his lonely exile on the island of Patmos. But, of course, this comfort was not for him alone. Revelation was recorded not to provide a hobby for future bored saints or a theological battlefield for contentious Christians, but as a means of encouragement for the church at war until 'the old order of things has passed away' (21:4). The aged apostle would hear the jubilant voices around the throne praising the Lamb who was slain, who, with His blood, had purchased multitudes 'from every tribe and language and people and nation' (5:9). He would then hear the deafening announcement, 'The kingdom of the world has become the kingdom of our Lord and of his Messiah, and he will reign for ever and ever' (11:15). Why else would men and women heroically continue to love and live for Jesus if there were no future hope? 'If only for this life we have hope in Christ, we are of all people most to be pitied' (1 Cor. 15:19).

A PEOPLE OF VISION

In these days, we need to live in our Bibles and also ladle encouragement into our souls through reading Christian biography. As we have sought to emphasize, the reading of Christian biography is essential as we drink in how earlier believers faced trial and temptation, and yet overcame difficulty and discouragement by God's limitless grace. If we jettison the life stories of those who have gone before, or consign them simply to history, we will sail into stormy seas lacking the ballast so needed to stabilize and sustain us. We need to seize every tool at our disposal that will enable us to keep the fire burning and our vision bright.

Having taken our brief stroll along the shelves of biography, let us ask why it was that those we read of—and many others beside, over the years—were willing to forsake the earthly comforts of home and loved ones, risking their lives, or, in some cases, even laying them down? Perhaps we could answer with one word: vision! A vision of God; a vision of the lost; a vision of the cross and its power; a vision given and fuelled by the Holy Spirit. And why do we continue to love and live for Jesus Christ when we know that life could be much easier if we didn't? The answer is exactly the same: vision.

AN ETERNAL GLORY

By faith, we have glimpsed the reality of eternity, and therefore our whole focus has shifted from the 'now' to the 'then', from the visible to the invisible; immortality, eternal life, the crown of righteousness—these are the things that motivate us now. Since the day we came to recognize who Jesus Christ is, we have been able to agree with Paul that 'our light and momentary troubles are achieving for us an eternal glory that far outweighs them all'. We then join him in the natural conclusion: 'So we fix our eyes not on what is seen, but on what is unseen, since what is seen is temporary, but what is unseen is eternal' (2 Cor. 4:17–18). Any suffering or sacrifice for Christ—no matter how great that might be—is nothing when compared with the glory that will one day be revealed. On one side we have the wisp of suffering; on the other, the weight of eternal glory. C. S. Lewis says, 'All the loneliness, angers, hatreds, envies and itchings that [this world] contains, if rolled into one single experience and put into the scale against the least moment of the joy that is felt in Heaven, would have no weight that could be registered at all.'[7] For this reason, we focus not on the ice of our discouragements, but endeavour to keep the flame of faith burning brightly.

IT'S OVER!

The day will soon be here when the battle will finally be over. The great deceiver, discourager and destroyer, and those who followed him, will be cast away—for ever (Rev. 20:10, 15). The conflict will have ended, and joyful, frenzied songs of victory will fill the air. All the saints will be gathered in, and in an atmosphere of ecstatic joy and worship, tales will be exchanged of battles fought and victories won—the bottom line for every one of them, of course, being how worthy the Lamb is to receive glory, honour and praise. 'And they shall be mine,' declares the Lord Almighty, 'in that day when I make up my jewels' (Mal. 3:17 KJV). His jewels! Sin-ruined men and women, redeemed and beautifully restored by Jesus, and all of grace! But, meanwhile, the battle below rages, and we fight on, not knowing for how many more days. *William Gurnall* spurs us on:

As part of Christ's army you march in the ranks of gallant spirits. Every one of your fellow soldiers is a child of the King. Some, like you, are in the midst of the battle, besieged on every side by affliction and temptation. Others, after many assaults, rebuffs and rallyings of their faith, are already standing upon the wall of heaven as conquerors. From there they look down and urge you, their comrades still on earth, to march up the hill after them. Their cry is, 'Fight to the death and the City is your own, as now it is ours! For the waging of a few days' conflict, you will be rewarded with heaven's glory. One moment of this celestial joy will dry up all your tears, heal all your wounds, and erase the sharpness of the fight with the joy of your permanent victory.'[8]

Perhaps today will be your last day of battle. So we boldly 'press on towards the goal to win the prize for which God has called [us] heavenwards in Christ Jesus' (Phil. 3:14). How wonderful it will be on that day to be able to cry triumphantly, with the great apostle, 'For to me, to live is Christ and to die is gain' (1:21)!

And on that day when my strength is failing
The end draws near and my time has come
Still my soul will sing Your praise unending
Ten thousand years and then forevermore.

(Matt Redman, '10,000 Reasons')

ICE AND FIRE

Notes

1 Mike Pilavachi, *Everyday Supernatural*, quoted on Twitter, @mikepilav, 31 January 2018

2 Calvin's *Commentary* on Lev. 6:9, BibleHub, https://biblehub.com/commentaries/calvin/leviticus/6.htm.

3 Matthew Henry, *Commentary on the Whole Bible*, on Lev. 6:8–13, Bible Hub, https://biblehub.com/commentaries/mhcw/leviticus/6.htm.

4 Arthur Matthews, *Born for Battle* (Sevenoaks: OMF Books, 1983), p. 73.

5 *The Collected Works of Samuel Chadwick*. Originally published in *The Way to Pentecost* (Berne, IN: Light and Hope Publications, 1932; Kindle edn), loc. 3173/3177.

6 *Christian Weekly News,* 26 September 2014.

7 C. S. Lewis, *The Great Divorce* (London: William Collins, 2013), pp. 122–123.

8 William Gurnall, *The Christian in Complete Armour* (Edinburgh: Banner of Truth, 1988), p. 27.

ICE AND FIRE